It's All Just A Sales Pitch
Why We Believe
What We Believe

*A fairly comprehensive excursion
through a rationally deduced explanation of
why we want what we want,
why we believe what we believe
and how others make us believe
what they want us to believe.*

by

Dave T. Garland III

For Kathy, the world's most supportive, tolerant, understanding, and loving wife. Your ceaseless encouragement continually inspires me to be better than I am. So thank you for providing the motivational sustenance that allowed me to spill all of these thoughts and ideas directly from my brain onto the pages. And thank you for the relentless provocation that ultimately produced a welcome finality to this project.

CONTENTS

INTRODUCTION 1

SECTION ONE
Being Trained to Believe
{Introductory Sales Pitch Education}

Chapter One
In the Beginning 7
Chapter Two
The End of 'It'. 19
Chapter Three
The Real Cool School Fool 33
Chapter Four
Oh Grow Up 60

SECTION TWO
Replacing Reality and Facts
With Opinions and Beliefs
{The Paradigms of Sales Pitching}

Chapter Five
Reality vs. Perception / Truth vs. Belief 77
Chapter Six
The Primal Forces of Nature 107
Chapter Seven
The Herd Mentality 129

SECTION THREE
The Pitch Masters
{Who, What, Why, How and When to Believe}

Chapter Eight
The Want Fulfilling Marketplace 159
Chapter Nine
God vs. Religion 188
Chapter Ten
Politics and the Law 204

SECTION FOUR
The Warping, Twisting and Perverting
of Perceptions and Beliefs
{The Art Of Deception}

Chapter Eleven
Self-Pitching 245
Chapter Twelve
The Magician's Tent 271
Chapter Thirteen
Using Your Brain Without Losing Your Mind . . 296

A Few Universal Maxims for
Human Life On Earth 309

Afterword 313

INTRODUCTION

Sales pitches permeate, influence and direct our lives from the moment we're born until the day we die. And, as the evidence will show, sales pitches are truly the origin of all mankind's opinions and beliefs. This book can serve as a simple guidebook to help restructure belief-based realities back into reality-based beliefs. It can also serve as a debunker manual. You know, to debunk some of the bunk that seems to dominate our beliefs. Only by reestablishing objective observational awareness can the mind maintain an unbiased and analytical thought process and ultimately restore personal sanity, (Or, at the very least, self-respect).

Could Abraham Lincoln really have been right? Can all of the people really be fooled some of the time? Can some of the people really be fooled all of the time? Or is it possible that all of the people can be fooled all of the time? The obvious answer to each of these questions is a resounding yes.

Belief manipulation is definitely the name of the game here. And the game is based on the reality that every human being eventually believes something. The daunting question is: Where do our "somethings" come from?

This book is for all whose brains haven't yet completely matured, or "manured," into the biased, closed-mindedness of self-absorbed adulthood. For those whose have (and the human brain is far from sedentary and steadfast, so clearly there's still hope), may this book serve as a tool to un-mature and un-manure the inner workings of your cluttered cerebral storage compartment.

What follows is an attempt to examine and expose the massive impact that "sales pitching" and "being sales-pitched" has on individuals, groups, nations and, ultimately, all of humanity. Why? Because sales pitches are, without a doubt, the source, the foundation, the structure and the actual cause of mankind's cumulative BS infested beliefs.

Most of what we know—or think we know—about reality originates from whatever we've filtered and absorbed through our five senses. Everything else we know comes from sales pitches, and when we apply mental thought processes to the combination of our sensory inputs along with all of the sales pitches, a whole bunch of opinions and beliefs begin to coalesce.

We all suffer, to some degree, from tightly held delusions brought about by our mental consumptions of other people's mental excretions.

Because human beings are creatures of comfort, we tend to believe or accept as truth whatever is comfortable to accept, and conversely we doubt or reject most of the information and beliefs that are uncomfortable. If you doubt this assertion, I apologize for your discomfort.

Nevertheless, the old adage, "People believe only what they want to believe" is based in truth and in human nature. After all, who would really maintain beliefs that, to them, are decidedly unbelievable?

Unbelievable beliefs are extremely uncomfortable for anyone to believe. There are, I suppose, masochistic believers. I assume these are the ones who perpetually believe their own doubts and then doubt their own beliefs.

One of the primary intentions of this literary expedition is to identify, or at least, expose the role that manipulation plays in the solidification of our deepest, most strongly held beliefs. My contention is that our beliefs are both a result of and a guiding force behind most of our mental comforts and discomforts.

What really validates a belief? Hopefully pursuing the answer to this question will shed at least some light on why our beliefs and doubts become so dear to us that we protect and defend them as entrenched facts, truths and realities.

What role does the "sales pitch" play in the makeup of the beliefs, viewpoints and values that we hold to be so sacred and irrefutable? And to what extent are these beliefs, viewpoints and values a true reflection of who we are?

To discover how we evolved into this bastion of beliefs and opinions we must go back to the very beginning. Really now, you don't seriously believe you dreamed up all of your beliefs on your own do you? Don't be silly, nobody is both that gifted and that egotistical, I hope.

The foundation most human exploitation is built on can be traced back to infancy. As you will see, the origin of life's voyage through the rolling waves of belief manipulation begins almost immediately with newborn "sales pitch training," which, as it turns out, is also the source of most of life's baggage.

What follows this initiation is a lifelong progression of sales pitch implemented belief indoctrinations. So we'll start at the very beginning and trace our enduring sales pitch-based belief dependence from its very source.

SECTION ONE

Being Trained to Believe
{Introductory Sales Pitch Education}

Chapter One
– In the Beginning –

Infantile Logic

Isn't labor a curious way to introduce a glorious new human life? "Labor." The word itself embodies so many negative connotations. In order to give birth, women must "go into labor" and have "labor pains." When "go into" and "pains" are added to labor, a word synonymous with work, toil, and effort, how can it be a pleasant experience for either the mother or the newborn?

The general response newborns give is a boisterous bellow. It's almost an extension of the ear numbing, delivery room "mommy screams" that even the loudest rock star would envy. From the newborn's perspective the situation is little more than an unexpected, unwelcome, coming-out party that interrupts the comfort of a warm, cozy, albeit cramped, fetal condo.

To most adults it's a slightly more complicated process. They see this as a procedure wrapped in moral and ethical issues, gender based value judgments, and, of course, the mystery of a father's inability to maintain any degree of cool in the delivery room. I certainly didn't.

Regardless of this ubiquitous pathway into existence, "it" (the newborn) successfully endures this rude awakening and, once again, another celebrated life begins.

> *Birth: when you and me, and all*
> *of the other he's and she's, first*
> *appear as nothing more than little*
> *"its." Henceforth, every cute,*
> *cuddly, chubby cheeked little know*
> *nothing newborn will be referred*
> *to as "it" (at least until "it" has*
> *matured enough to deserve a less*
> *demeaning moniker).*

This innocent babe is callously dragged, kicking and screaming, into a strange new realm only to be further assaulted by a disquieting flurry of bright lights, commotion, and noise. But these minor inconveniences are not in vane, because the world is blessed with yet another miniature bundle of human potential.

In most cases there are others around: doctors, nurses, and a mother to be sure. But this newest addition to the population doesn't know these people. Doesn't even know they are people. Yep, as far as "it" is concerned, this first worldly experience is an unfamiliar cluster of pulling, poking, and wiping.

Yet, even with the perpetual bombardment of new sensations, newborns get over it pretty quickly. Most are cool with the whole scene, primarily because they don't know squat, not yet at least. Squat (n. [skwɵt] do-do, poo-poo). [1]

Squat is one of the very first sales pitch lessons in what will eventually be a lifetime filled with other crappy sales pitches. Making squat, along with peeing, sucking, and crying, becomes a force that enables this miniature human to completely control the actions of even the most intelligent and experienced adult.

This diminutive Churchill lookalike emerges into the world without any expectations. There are no visions of grandeur, no fantasies of success, or majestic goals to pursue, or worthwhile employment opportunities for that matter. The concept of a future itself is nonexistent. We're talking clean slate here. Having been abruptly severed from a modest life-support cord, this wee little creature is forced to successfully engage a self-contained breathing apparatus without the assistance of an instruction manual.

Mother Nature generously provides almost every child with this instinctual function. *Mother Nature? That's right, two mothers for each kid.* These two mothers, along with the attending support team, generously and enthusiastically supply most of life's basic necessities. The kid does the rest; suck in some sustenance, process, poop,

---

[1] *This shouldn't to be confused with "crap"—something completely different and abundantly supplied by other people in due course.*

pee, and puke. Pretty complicated stuff scientifically, but not really any big deal to a newborn. That is, as long as there is always something life sustaining to suck on. The reality is that newborns are completely dependent on the boobs they are faced with. As circumstance would have it, this dependency exists in one form or another all throughout life

We all start out in relatively the same way, as cute, chubby cheeked little putzes. A lifelong struggle for control begins about here. It begins with magic, or at least the illusion of magic. While physiologically impossible there is a phenomenon that has existed throughout the history of mankind: i.e., almost every clueless infant comes equipped with the ability to wrap a full grown adult around its little finger.

> *"This is so cool, when I cry I get food*
> *and when I cry again they clean up*
> *all that smelly squat stuff."* [2]

To the kid, this is wonderful, total dependence yet total control. Residing now in a perfect world of delusional self-absorption. What else in life could this bundle of joy possibly need? But hey, this sense of control isn't the kid's fault. It's obviously the adult's doing. Aren't they the ones who train themselves to do whatever the kid wants? Who's subservient now? Hapless parents can't figure out why the little brat would become so relentlessly demanding.

---

[2] *That was baby thoughts not real quotes. But wouldn't it be great if we had been able to verbalize our newborn thoughts with an adult vocabulary?*

Wow, what an ironic cause-effect paradox. Parents actually show "it" how to push their buttons and then get frustrated with those constant annoying cries for attention. Either that, or all babies are born with a sadistic sense of humor that motivates them to intentionally interrupt the parent's quiet slumber at all hours of the night.

This control conditioning is the first, parent-sponsored, Newborn Sales Pitch Training Course or more specifically, Getting What You Want by Manipulation: 101. This is a perfect testing environment for the kid, because it involves the ultimate captive audience. This little bundle of demand has a rapidly developing brain, so these courses in "getting" are life's initial mental steps down life's bumpy sales pitch road.

This sales pitch training is the key to keeping others occupied with satisfying every personal want and need. It is the beginning of a quest for life's true purpose, i.e., to maintain an everlasting state of pleasure while completely avoiding any possibility of pain or discomfort. Better known as getting everything you want while never giving up anything—one of the principal purposes of most sales pitches. You have probably heard this misguidedly referred to as "happiness." At least this is generally what most of us were pitched as happiness early in life.

In a slightly more advanced elementary sales pitching class, "it" will eventually learn to cultivate and hone the skills necessary to not only manipulate but to direct, influence and ultimately control in order to satisfy its own selfish purpose. The only obstacle will be an unavoidable human predisposition to fall for the sales pitches of "others." And, as sure as "it" will soon become responsible for dealing with its own squat, "it" will inevitably succumb to other people's sales pitch crap.

Sales pitches take on many forms in early life. They run from the sincere, helpful and supportive to the ruthless, maniacal and deceptive. To be sure, sales pitches from these "others" will be forceful, enticing, relentless and, to a large degree, overwhelming. This is the "crap" referred to earlier that will undoubtedly produce most of life's trials and tribulations.

The only thing that really matters at this point is to be properly attended to, and therein lies the sustenance-based needs that no one can live without. And so, as with all newborns, "it" sucks. Yes, "it" sucks, therefore "it" lives. Once again, a reference to the boobs everyone is faced with in order to survive.

Days pass and these fundamental techniques of survival slowly mature into the elementary pain/avoidance and pleasure/gratification attainment techniques.

"God, when I don't suck for a long time I am really uncomfortable, and this squat stuff is even starting to offend me."

Initial up-bringers, through their loving concern and inability to cope with the little rascal's relentless and boisterous demands, are almost eager to give into these not-so-subtle control techniques. Now, like they say, what goes around comes around. There soon comes a time when the infantile pitching process is rudely countermanded by an adult counter pitch. The earliest experience in being counter pitched is most often provided by the folks (or up-bringers). These up-bringers are equipped with their own not-so-delicate manipulation weapons, not the least of which is deprivation.

The use of the word "no" becomes one of the most hated, and sometimes feared, tactics that any of us ever encounter. The "no" response increasingly subjects all tots to a brutal denial of expected comforts. Of course this leads to a rebellion that results in bloodcurdling, high-pitched frequencies in total disproportion to the tiny lungs that produced them. This is what infants consider an effective and perfectly reasonable "sales pitch" response. This reaction is justifiable because, to "it," "no" is a totally unfair and unjust tactic. After all, these are the same people that set the rules that "it" would never be denied.

"How could they do this to me and why are they hassling me with this crap? They are the ones who taught me that I'm in control, and I get what I want when I want it."

This is where "no" is a device of seeming torture. It is employed gradually and harmlessly enough at first. The more forceful and frequent the demands are, the more intense the deprivation. But hey, not to worry, it gets even worse.

This deteriorating sense of control slowly evolves into an unthinkable reality. What follows is vigorous and relentless subservience training. This new reality becomes more invasive with each passing day. "It" gets what "it" wants gradually evolves into "it" only gets what "they" want. This cruelty that tikes must endure is known as "discipline." It's a good thing infants are small. If they possessed any effective degree of strength their initial reactions to most forms of discipline would be to tear the house apart. It's bad enough they employ tantrums. I believe this is where an old term for parenting originated. Over the years this term evolved from "child rear-ing" to "child rearing," where rear-ing meant a good old whack in the fanny. Many people today even find the term "discipline" offensive or invasive. *Maybe they weren't properly reared.*

Okay, exactly what has gone on here? Well, the fact is, this child is being indoctrinated to a conditioned response. "It" in turn will instill many conditioned responses in ma, pa, Aunty Nell and, of course, the clueless babysitter. This is the essence of early infant sales pitching.

During this early development of a child's brain the synapses and neurotransmitter activity begins to form behavioral patterns. These behavioral patterns become almost totally focused on manipulation of others in order to satisfy the insatiable cravings for both necessities and comforts. The employment of these conditioned response patterns is the very foundation of what we all know as manipulation.

Having children of my own, I referred to this manipulation as a "parent trap." Later in life, many grow out of this condition of responding to the conditioning of their conditioned responses—or so I've heard. I'm pretty sure my kids still haven't fully divested themselves of this form of manipulation. With apologies, I, being a typical father, can attest to the extraordinary energy and effort my wife put into repairing all of the "spoiled child" character flaws I implanted into our poor, impressionable children. I still feel like I was duped into doing it. I did give into their sales pitches sometimes, well, maybe most of the time. Okay, okay, almost every time.

Another World

Even while the torture of becoming both dependent and acquiescent manifests itself, another unexpected life-changing day shatters this self-centered realm. It is that day when "it" is confronted with a horror so great that life itself will be forever affected. *"Oh my God, my parents and I aren't the only ones in the world."* These are the "others" that creep into "it's" world almost without warning. *"Whoa, wait a second now. Who were these freaky coochy-cooers?"* Or, worse yet, *"Who or what is that other "it"?* Well, these are the ubiquitous babbling aliens and the annoying little attention stealers.

One of the earliest exhibitions of the threat response is when "it" is eventually left alone with one or more of these blithering idiots. In pre-speech infant lingo the typical reaction is, *"My life source has abandoned me!"* or *"Quick, give me something to suck on."* What does any of this have to do with sales pitches? Well, from now on and for the rest of "it's" life, "it" will be at the mercy of, or at least dependent on, both the humanity and inhumanity of these "others." The resulting certainty is that "others" will eventually want to manipulate "it" into doing, thinking or, more importantly, believing what they want. Sorry kid, from now on it's nothing but a brutal and unyielding world of human "sales pitch" manipulation.

We have all been there. Our circumstances may be varied but the results were the same. In time we all either reluctantly grew accustom to the annoying influence of these bozos or we futilely rebelled and physically resisted.

Fortunately, out of sheer self-preservation, "it" begins to cultivate a slightly more advanced or sophisticated set of defenses to shield against the annoying manipulation maneuvers of "others." Through trial and error, rote learning and boisterous temper tantrums "it" eventually becomes adept at developing its own sales pitches that generate escape routes from the unrelenting irritation and inattention that "others" seem to revel in administering. These include the incessant screaming at others who actually believe that holding this precious bundle is desirable or appreciated, or the classic slapping of the hand into the bowl of some vile concoction that baby food makers peddle as palatable. The latter is most effective when maximum trajectory of the darkest colored mush creates a pattern on light colored clothing or curtains. Both plum and beet flavors work really well.

Dissatisfaction can take many forms. When applied often and repeatedly, most "others" are generally bright enough to give into an infant's desires. Some more feeble-minded "others" even become perpetually susceptible to "its" demands, particularly the babysitters, but only the ones who actually bother to care.

Now I don't personally remember, but I've been told that I would shimmy over the prison bars of my crib in a desperate struggle to elude the evil forces of those who would impose their will on me. I like to interpret this as my personal attempt at the shrewd, "You left me alone, what was I supposed to do?" or "You can't keep me cooped up, I'm a thrill-seeking adventurer" sales pitches. More probably this was my non-linguistic endeavor to communicate displeasure with persistent attempts to stifle my curiosity. Nonetheless, it was certainly one of my more futile attempts at imposing my will on the folks. And imposing one's will is certainly one of the more overt forms of sales pitching.

Speaking Of An Imposing Poser

Sooner or later, another "it" enters the scene. A temporary curiosity goes into full operational mode. "My God, what is that and what is it doing in my world?" An intense wide-eyed inquisitive glare results in a momentary standoff, but this mutual interest quickly diminishes into a playful or curious apathy.

Fortunately, curiosity and threat perception seem to last only a short time at this age. But then something totally unexpected happens. The other "it" is given attention by one of the "others." Then the survival defense mechanism once again kicks in. *"Back off, jerk. All of that attention you're getting belongs to me."* This initial response is followed by the ever popular, and still effective, attention-demanding tantrum sales pitch. *"Don't you dare give that little twerp my food or playthings, and, for God's sake, pay attention to me."*

We all start out pretty much the same way. We learn that both whining and complaining will not only satisfy our demands, they are really the catalyst that can most effectively maintain focus on us. Throughout life, more effective manipulation techniques will be learned, developed and perfected, but some among us will never be completely weaned from the grease that a good old squeaky wheel tantrum can provide. Once you learn that yelling is effective, it's hard to break the habit.

Chapter Two
– The End of "IT" –

Thus Begins the Even More Irritating Age of "I," "I," "I" and "Me," "Me," "Me."

"It" is now maturing, or is at least morphing, into something just beyond a hapless heap of potential. This is a transformation into the earliest version of "I," "me," "us" and "we."

Henceforth, depending on how defaming it is in context, "it" will be replaced by "you," "they" or "them." This will be done without prejudice or intentional personal insult but rather for the sake of clarity and simplicity, so please don't take offense. That being said, I do not envy your position. I simply feel that you are, undoubtedly, more capable of dealing with degradation than I would ever be. Now there are limits to this personal abuse. So, to be fair, I will also occasionally refer to "I" and "me" in either reflective anecdotes or personally flattering circumstances as a form of reparation and self- deprecating atonement. Hopefully you won't garner too much enjoyment or gratification from my self-imposed exposure to personal humiliation. I grant you this is not a very professional use of literary application. But, alas, just as in life, we will all be exploited as the subjects, perpetrators, victims, heroes and, of course, the villains of both ridicule and praise just as "it" was in the first chapter. Or at least this is another part of my sales pitch

Now you're probably asking yourself: Why continue this journey through the early years of human experience? Well, because it is during these really early years that the brain is susceptible to the developmental and imprinting patterns of belief absorption and the involuntary predisposition to belief dependence and reliance. The very early exposure to judgments of what is right vs. what is wrong, what is good vs. what is bad, as well as which patterns of conduct are acceptable or unacceptable will influence, or even direct, future behavior for many years to come. (I say "exposures to" because, obviously, few of us actually behave as if we know the difference between right and wrong.)

Moreover, how and when to react to other people's commands and desires, as well as how to elicit personal wants and needs from others, are seeds that are planted at this very early stage. Unfiltered beliefs are implanted into vulnerable little brains that haven't yet developed the skills necessary to employ healthy skepticism. With no established ability to rationally judge, all input is interpreted as truth or fact. Kind of like how we judge our favored political candidates. For some, an entire lifetime will be spent believing a bunch of idiotic ramblings they were exposed to during this mentally innocent period. The healthy skepticism that is necessary for human survival will, slowly but surely, begin to be developed during the upcoming painful and irritating adolescent and educational periods.

Now, as you grow physically, it becomes a struggle to maintain your manipulation effectiveness. While you continuously attempt to develop new and more strategically effective exploitation tactics to extract what you want from the "others," they employ their own tactical countermeasures. In the ever-popular dietary preference example, parents rarely stand a chance. To counter parental countermeasures you usually resort to the ever-compelling "food choice displeasure tantrum" opposition pitch. This involves a vigorous attempt to redirect objectionable food to a destination other than your mouth. The bigger the mess on your face, the floor and the server, the more you revel in a giggling victory celebration. The folks rapidly buy into this and not only do you win but you rarely experience that particular "Gerber" again. Admit it now, didn't it feel good to be in control during this youthful period?

Toddler Babble Talk and "Loco" Motion

Crawl you little devil—crawl. Free at last, free at last, thank God almighty you are—

"Whoa. What the—Put me down. Wait a minute, I'm sure I was going somewhere."

Of course you have no idea where, but by some miracle of nature you are on the move, able to mop the floor with both hands and knees.

You rejoice in your newfound ability to gather a vast collection of dirt and germs as you unthinkingly scramble on your mystical journeys. You are oblivious to what should be total discomfort as you scurry along all decked out in your cushy diaper full of wee-wee and squat. Isn't it great that instead of just sitting in it, you can now lug it around with you? Initially it makes you feel warm all over. Well, probably not all over. But you do eventually become aware of the shortcomings brought on by hauling around your mobile latrine.

As your world continues to evolve, new tactics must be both developed and employed in order to facilitate your efforts to perpetually re-center the world around you. What's a child to do?

"I still want all of the attention I deserve. The rest of the time I'd like everyone to just leave me alone so I can discover new ways to injure myself. After all, I've got curiosity kicking in, and it needs my attention."

Your new perplexing dilemma is how to get ma, pa and the "others" on board with your newly evolved set of needs. Armed with only your cuteness and your delusion of personal achievement, no matter how minuscule, the crusade for "me, me, me" is still paramount. Your challenge is how to preserve the highest degree of attention while maintaining your ever-expanding realm of independence.

"Ah-ha, attention; the comforting reward they give me for performing some brainless act they think is cute. And when that isn't effective enough, thank goodness my royal fit performance still works."

Either way, the goal of being spoiled rotten must be achieved at any cost.

Consequently, a paradox is created.

"I must accomplish this goal of maintaining perpetual attention while being left alone to create my own trouble."

Careful partner, there's a precipitous cliff at the end of that path.

"Ah ha, where to find a precipitous cliff?"

(I must compliment you on your adolescent mental vocabulary.)

"Now let me see. Danger, yea, that's it. Danger really seems to bring them running. I'm sure there is something really stupid I can do to center their attention on me, without getting smacked in the rear of course."

(No one ever said that sales pitches have to be smart or void of pain.) Bam. "What was that noise?" No worries, it was only the hair dryer hitting the floor. They must have purposely left the cord dangling irresistibly just within reach.

"Did I do that? I must have cuz here they come. Man, it feels great to still be in control."

Fortunately, this four-point floor scramble method is short lived. Besides, the "others" all use the two-leg system and they can all reach the more dangerous stuff. So, while your tongue is being trained to produce acceptable sounds, you might as well discover the pitfalls of gravity and balance. If God had meant for humans to stand, he would have given us four legs. This would obviously counter the propensity that every one of us has to perpetually fall on our face.

The Ever-evolving Little Demon

You've got legs and can now experience an elevated lifestyle. So stand tall and waddle. You're reaching a whole new level now, albeit not a very high level. Still, it does afford a more advantageous perspective.

"How could they ignore me now? How could they possibly withhold their adoration and pride? Wait a second now, what do you mean 'Stay away from this' and 'Don't touch that?'"

Don't worry that's just the folks sales pitching you on a bunch of arbitrary safety and survival skills. Yes, all of the threats, warnings, and attempts to instill fear, direction and advice are all just the folks trying to bring you up right. But you never let that deter you.

Besides, they only employ these not-so-subtle forms of sales pitches to infuse a sense of what is right and wrong. When you rapidly waddle toward the basement stairs, two alternative methods of learning right from wrong are available. The first is for ma or pa to convince you that choosing an alternative destination would be a wise lesson in "right." The second is a head-over-heels tumble down into a painful lesson in "wrong."

Either method has its advantages, but remember, any time you are being convinced, regardless of the context, you are being sales-pitched. Still, you do ultimately progress safely through your physically and mentally demanding diminutive years. You make it through, in spite of frequently ignoring a great deal of the well-meaning orders and advice of those who care about you. Don't let this achievement go to your head. Most people make it through life the same way. That's certainly how I did it.

Behavioral expectations and reinforcement, prejudicial viewpoint imprinting and the long-lasting foundations of bias are all imposed somewhere during this period of vulnerable immaturity. Infants are perpetually bombarded with beliefs. They are blissfully unaware that these subconsciously planted attitudes will become the foundation of their own fundamental beliefs.

Beliefs of others will ultimately influence personal bias, gender typecasting, conformity expectations, religious direction, along with a mixture of human stereotyping and a myriad of other prejudices. Bet ya never thought about that back when you were a kid, did ya? I know it certainly never occurred to me—even when it was being beaten into me. I mean really, why would anyone care about any of that crap when conscious attention is being focused on putting one stubby little foot in front of the other without falling over?

Toddlers don't just hear parental commands. They're also extremely sensitive to the positive and negative attitudes or the angry and heated emotions behind the gobbledygook. Toddlers hear and see almost everything that's going on. Of course they don't understand any of it, but they are influenced by the daily repetition and all of the attitudes within their field of awareness. The hungry minds of youth will absorb negative parental attitudes right along with the well-intentioned loving messages. Even when they are focused on I, I, I, and me, me, me, they are subconsciously cognizant of ambient information and attitudes.

Don't you find it ironic and a bit little strange that the advice and direction sales pitches that you ignored during your early years are the ones you either already have or will almost certainly perpetrate on your own kids? I know my kids certainly made an exerted effort to ignore all of the same things I ignored. Serves me right.

The Sibling Jerk

A sibling is merely a perpetual attention-sucking annoyance. It is an incredibly irritating form of competition that never seems to diminish. Oh sure, the sibling coexists with a somewhat tolerable degree of compatibility at times, but the paranoia brought on by possession security disrupts any possibility of a truly trusting relationship.

The only redeeming quality of a sibling is that when some terrible misdeed is perpetrated, the blame can be redirected to the sibling. This maneuver can expand any child's sales pitch capabilities. Unfortunately, this ploy can also backfire when "it" becomes the victim of this little blame game. The innocent faced, "I didn't do it" sales pitch immediately comes back into play. As I remember it, almost everything I was blamed for was my brother's fault.

The initial exposure to another "it" is one of a child's first glimpses into a whole new world. When someone else is introduced, this poor naive little kid is now relegated to surviving in the often strange and irritating realm of "we." In order to make a relatively painless and successful passage into this new territory there are inevitable conditions that must now be dealt with. Along with the requisite competition for attention, there is now competition for toys, junk, territory and a whole bunch of other really important stuff. You know, that stuff you really didn't want until a sibling or some other little brat wanted it.

A rivalry-based hatred and instinctual distrust of these other little twerps is enough to force any little nipper into a continuous endeavor to be more accepted than this unwelcome competition. This sought-after acceptance is initially obtained primarily by exhibiting all the wonderful and awesome attributes that the kid has to offer.

Obviously these attributes are far superior to those displayed by any of the other attention-grabbers out there. Naturally, they are, in their own selfish way, apathetic toward these magnificent personal attributes. They prefer to flaunt their own unwelcome virtues and qualities. Thus begins the lifelong ebb and flow of, "Look at me, I'm important," and, "No, no, look at me, I'm more important." This is undoubtedly the seed of various social sales pitches as well as most over-inflated egos.

At this point there is another small but important developmental transition. Enter now into the era of the tantrum. Within this tantrum sanctum, far more aggressive and uncompromising battle plans of "I want" and "I get" are concocted. This is sometimes referred to as the "terrible twos," and it is the epitome of a toddler's demand-based sales pitching. It is during these trying times that potty training also rears its compulsory head. (Yes, this is an extremely immature pun. Be forewarned, in spite of my best efforts, these involuntary mental hiccups sometimes migrate directly from my brain onto the page.)

The initial mental response to potty training goes something like this: "You want me to do what? Where? ... You're kidding, right?" Now we all know that early potty training is really the parent's shrewd effort to reduce child-rearing costs by eliminating diaper expenses from the budget.

Best Friends?

Finding a best friend at this age is easy because most kids have extremely low standards. If you are constantly around lots of "others," one of them will eventually stick out as acceptable. In most cases this happens simply by chance. If there is only a couple to choose between, you have a far better chance of choosing the wrong one.

Remember, you still have no social judgment skills. Either way, almost everyone ends up with a friend who they deem more tolerable than any of the other bozos, or bozettes. Friends are important at this age. They are the compatriots you don't need to perpetually pitch. They don't really have too much stuff that you want anyway. The best thing is they are generally content with not pitching you. Unfortunately, the dynamics of best friend relationships changes drastically as you grow older.

Learning How to Want

Somewhere between the adjustment to a "non-diaper" fashion ensemble and the "tie-your-own-shoes" learning experience, you find it necessary to refine your comfort demand parameters. There are so many new things to like or dislike at this age that it becomes more difficult to convey your specific desires. How to voice your approval or disapproval now requires a more mature vocabulary, or any vocabulary at all. Your parents are eternally thankful you haven't yet mastered the linguistic abilities necessary to specifically describe your every desire. Put another way, you haven't developed the sales pitch techniques or requisite vocabulary that would enable you to acquire everything you want. This does, however, also create a frustration felt by both you and your parents. After all, they do comprise the limited supply side of your unlimited demand side.

When you are led by the hand through the toy store, it's easy to point and yell, "I want." Without a vast array of available choices to randomly point at, verbalizing something specific becomes a little more restraining.

When there's nothing to choose between, you are forced to put forth the strenuous mental effort required to come up with something actually worth wanting. At this age, mastering the lingo that could provide you with every little thing you think you want would make you a complete sales pitch prodigy.

In a situation like this you would also discover that getting everything you want through manipulation, teaches you that you don't have to work for what you want. I believe this is the format of the instruction manual for shysters, impostors, swindlers, con artists and, of course, politicians, lawyers and hedge fund managers. Oh what a fruitful character-building life lesson that would provide. If you are the offspring of the top 1 percent you can obviously ignore this entire last paragraph.

A sales pitch tool is introduced during this period of your life that becomes one of the most vital instruments in your little survival kit of demand techniques. It is, however, a little uncomfortable until you get the hang of how and when to use it.

It's a tool that requires you to assume a somewhat subservient position in order to obtain your wants from those in charge. It is that ever-powerful and compelling word "please." It's really more of a weapon than a tool. It is almost indefensible when properly employed. Once it's tactfully utilized it is unparalleled in its ruthless effectiveness. "Please" is quite possibly the most influential sales pitch force available to any child.

"No," of course, grows to be the dreaded sales pitch destroyer. Whenever the "no" tactic is deployed you can, and often do, revert back to your old typical fallback default sales pitch response, the tantrum. You are, after all, still in your "brat" years. This "please" scheme is effective, because the temperament in which it is presented is so utterly contrary to the usual obnoxious tone of your demands. Your befuddled parents are left with few defenses.

You, because you're such a devious imp, only utilize this magic word when you really, really want something so desperately that you temporarily abandon your typical devilish ways. There's simply no way to employ the "please" tactic unless you are polite. This is sometimes difficult because, after all, you, and everyone else at this age, are all still just self-serving brats. No worries though, everyone eventually grows out of it, well, almost everyone.

Once the fundamental techniques of acquiring your basic wants are mastered, or at least persistently tested, you are free to experiment with the frolicsome activities that employ a higher level of "discomfort avoidance" and "pleasure attainment." Loneliness, failure, rejection and your irritating relatives become the primary objects of avoidance. Your essential attainment pursuits become companionship, success and, of course, social acceptance.

These are the slightly higher levels of the comfort/discomfort parameters that the remainder of your juvenile life will be committed to balancing. Unfortunately, once again, the "others" really couldn't care less. They will be too busy employing their own selfish attempts at redirecting your attention away from your stupid little goals so you can focus on them. You are also entering that really amusing phase where your overall level of control decreases, but your ability to either cause or get into even more trouble increases exponentially.

Chapter Three
– The Real Cool School Fool –

School, Cool?

A young life progresses rapidly—if you call this life. But, hey, still no responsibilities. Up until now, most people's minds have been made up (or made up for them) before they've had a chance to learn how to think, let alone apply rational thought. With this condition now firmly established, you can gleefully and naively enter the realm of formal education, clinging tightly to the mental baggage of an accumulation of your parentally imposed beliefs. The cerebral minefield has now been set and is primed to explode most of these beliefs.

Ah, the pre-school years. It's the beginning of a warm and wonderful stage of life. It is a time of learning, giving, caring and the embracing of many close and fulfilling relationships. Oh please, give me a break.

In reality this is when you realize that your primary responsibility is to keep all of these jerks away from your stuff, except for the ones that you, in your vast time-tested judgment, deem worthy. While you may never admit it, you only consider a select few worthy because they, in their own warped adolescent judgment, reciprocally find you somewhat acceptable.

Like a lamb being led to slaughter, your prepubescent mind now enters the socially competitive arena of pitching and pitch deflecting. Now, add to this your undeveloped abilities to accurately interpret reality or decipher good from bad, right from wrong, reality from fantasy, truth from lies or fact from fiction.

There is also a lack of the fundamental skills necessary to apply rational thought to opinion-based pitches that are presented as certainties. Now you know why there are so many screwed up kids and why most of them hate school. Is anyone up for a little pain avoidance? Sorry kids, this is social enlightenment by scholastic entrapment. Is there no one to provide an avenue of escape?

Salvation Is at Hand

Most youngsters are endowed with a large degree of curiosity and, at least, a small propensity for mischief. The mischief part is obviously an effort to push the limits of the painful edge of the learning curve. On the curiosity side, kids learn in spite of the inadequacies of modern teaching methods.

No matter how hard they fight it, directionless and clueless elementary school students absorb information like a sponge. Not so much formal education or useful knowledge, but a bunch of information nonetheless. Most retain only a minuscule amount of the purely academic information, and never dare question it when it's presented.

Why? Well it's not because they're dumb. No, it's because, so far, they haven't had enough practice at being smart. They haven't had to. Their brains are still pretty much empty, so there's plenty of space to cram in stuff like knowledge, experience and a bunch of other debris that's supposed to make them smart. The way it really works is that the majority of information is obtained from their peers and, obviously, most of this is misinformation. One thing, academically learned, is that the short-term comfort of not doing homework is eventually replaced by the embarrassing discomfort that ensues when it's due. Personally, I learned immeasurably more from little league, swim team and piano lessons than I did from any of my elementary school classroom instruction.

Sadly, during these impressionable school years, all information and misinformation, fact or fiction, is pretty much believed equally. Even worse, most of the misinformation accumulates and is stored in the brain as credible or reliable truths. Remember the "crap" that was referenced earlier? This is a lot of it.

What a Popular Little Cuss

During this period, it's also vitally important the proper use of cuss words is learned. Knowledge of the effective use of profanity can sometimes be the only release available to deal with all the crap piling up in a cluttered young mind.

Cursing also helps to alleviate the frustration and anger brought on by "others." Besides, it's really fun saying words that aren't supposed to be said. It also has the added benefit of impressing your peers with your ability to utilize this non-conforming language in order to fit in with them. It makes you a big hit with your gang of pals, or whatever faction of misfits you hang out with. And that, after all, is one of the primary purposes of a sales pitch.

The use of profanity is also a really fun and entertaining way to mitigate the fear, anxiety and frustration that dealing with the swarms of new attention hoarders present. Besides, you've heard older people cuss, so it must be cool, and cuss words that can make you cool must have superpowers. And what better way is there to express anger and pain?

Accumulating Trash

Human beings were programed, through evolution, to believe. It is much more comfortable for the human brain to believe than to doubt. This is a condition that has been proven repeatedly in scientific, and some not-so-scientific studies over the years. So, without a fully developed mental filtration system these "social students" are unable to decipher the validity of this profusion of "education" that bombards them. By default they're left with no choice.

They accept as fact most of the rubbish that's mixed

in with the information salad that is perpetually being served. This rubbish will remain in the human brain disguised as facts until experience exposes it for what it really is. At that time it will either be thrown out with some of the other accumulated trash or replaced with what is felt to be a more comfortable set of unreliable "facts."

Now you, because you are above average in intelligence, rapidly progress out of this naive, innocent and gullible stage. Still, in spite of an advanced intellect, your brain will remain riddled with the residue of this mental refuse for a very long time. Just as arteries slowly build up plaque because of what you choose to consume, your brain also continues to accumulate additional mental rubbish along the way. But unlike heart attacks, brain attacks result in rational thought and logic damage rather than heart damage. This is also why it is so incredibly difficult to convince yourself that, in spite of your tenacious grip on your opinions, you must doubt something that has been a longstanding belief. This lingering residue will have an influence on your belief system for a good part of your life.

A significant portion of your moral values, right/wrong ideals, beliefs/disbeliefs, political bias and religious influences are prejudiced to a large extent by this residual brain pollution. Throughout your academic years, the seeds planted in your mental garden will often yield noxious mischievous weeds right along with flowers of wisdom.

Nonetheless, during this period in your life, the scars you receive on your knees and elbows will heal long before those that pollute your brain. The neurons and chemicals in your brain form patterns that can remain intact for most of your life. This is also a product or result of your DNA, i.e., how you process information and not which information you choose to process. The effective sales pitches take place in the "what you choose to process," rather than the hereditary "how you process."

Just Another World Without Responsibilities

Yes, your school is a world of comfort where you spend your time either sitting in a classroom trying to stay awake or reading lots of books in an effort to expand your mind. Unfortunately, while you are indeed expanding your mind, you are doing it with what is primarily a bunch of scholastic fodder.

You aren't really filling up the old mental retention pond with real life knowledge. Other than some required preliminary academic "facts" that the remainder of your short career as a student will be based on, you aren't significantly advancing your ability to think. *If you can tell me the detailed facts you learned from the third chapter of your first algebra book, you have totally squandered what could have been a colorful and memorable time at school.*

You quickly discover that school is a world where the real learning goes on outside of class. It's kind of the key period of your social dexterity development. It is the first communal environment where you learn to quickly transition from pitching to being pitched and back again.

What an exciting time in your life. It's a warm and tender interlude that shelters you from the harshness of the real world. Sort of—well, not really—okay, not at all. Actually, it's more of a laid-back combat zone where you are forced into restricted quarters with an assortment of irritating overachievers, strange misfits, geeks and losers. It is a mishmash of juvenile humanity that will serve as an unavoidable mob you must now perpetually attempt to socialize with. The absurdity is that it is this mob's members who will ultimately determine your level of social acceptance.

Your school is really nothing more than a cramped little battlefield where you are confined with a judgmental legion of immature "others" that aren't of your choosing. These are the peers who you must now battle with in the personality-stifling arena of "Who am I smarter than?" "Who am I stronger than?" "Who am I cooler than?" and "Why should I care about studying when that one over there is so incredibly cute?"

Rejection Is Death

At some point acceptance by individuals within this schoolhouse mob becomes critical. As disturbing as this is, assimilation becomes a necessity that is commensurate with breathing, eliminating pimples and not embarrassing yourself in front of that incredibly cute one. Acceptance is one of the initial requirements that will ultimately define your social identity.

Without acceptance you are left with, God forbid, yourself. You've been there, done that, and you know how unsatisfying being alone with you can sometimes be. Even the possibility of the dull, dreary companionship of just you is excruciating. Unfortunately, this takes place just about the time the new and exciting brain-pleasing experience of dopamine dependence begins to apply its firm and lasting grip on your vulnerable and unsuspecting mind. It becomes a self-imposed responsibility to impress others while still being impressionable that creates a confusing and conflicting paradox.

Successful social assimilation is so essential during this period that it almost becomes your purpose for living. Why? Well, first, and least importantly, no one would benefit from all that awesome wonderfulness you exude. More significantly, without peer acceptance, you are deprived of the one thing that every good citizen has been trained to truly crave: status. This involves a myriad of socially based sales pitches, counter pitches. Status is that distorted window through which the "others" envision or determine your worth.

Up until now you have formed your own distinct image of yourself. You have pretty much acquiesced to your own self-image, no matter how inaccurate, self-deprecating or self-adulating. This untested self-imposed self-perception precludes you from accurately assigning your own social rank, so you find yourself at the mercy of these juvenile bozos. You are left vulnerable to indiscriminate judgmental assaults from those within the fickle schoolyard mob.

By way of rejection they have the power to strip you of both self-esteem and self-confidence. You acutely comprehend your vulnerability and primp like mad to make a favorable impression. After all, you still lack the requisite verbal communication skills necessary to define yourself to them. So, in order to best represent yourself to this band of jackals, you must, employ every one of your awkward efforts to impress them. Your "awkward efforts to impress" are tantamount to a "juvenile sales pitch" that desperately pleads for their approval.

This quest for recognition also requires that you repress any reliance on the exceedingly subjective opinion of your primary acceptance base, the folks. In my case, lacking the requisite academic level of achievement, I chose athletics as my primary route to acceptance. My secondary route was an all-out persistent effort directed at attempting to be the nicest guy in school. This second route never really worked out all that well. In my attempt to be accepted, I was so perpetually nice to everyone that I even irritated myself.

The dopamine in your brain is kicking in more often now. Dopamine indulges the beliefs and serves up pleasure. Dopamine is both the brain's pleasure drug and the brain's belief drug. Your dopamine is telling you to crave the pleasure and avoid the pain. The anticipation of socially inflicted pain is, in far too many cases, the reason behind some really stupid decisions. Bullying, revenge, retribution, stalking, physical violence and even suicide are some of the extreme measures employed by teens to mitigate their social difficulties. This pain of a social stigma, or even the possibility of rejection, has taken many lives, both literally and figuratively.

Thankfully, either through some miracle of nature or your sparkling and magnetic personality, someone eventually accepts you. This process of peer approval welcomes you into the pleasurable world of "conformity-ville." This includes clicks, clubs, gangs, frats, sororities and even informal or disorganized groupings. Misfits and rebels also conform to, and are accepted by, other misfits and rebels. These are the nonconformists who ultimately conform to the mutually accepted norms of their faction's adherence to nonconformity. The only rule in "conformity-ville" is that you must, at some level, conform in order to socially "fit in." Conform or the conformists will ostracize you.

Don't feel bad, we all give in somewhere. Life necessitates that each of us be accepted by at least one other human being, if not, then maybe by a computer or a pet. Of course this latter type of acceptance is obtainable only if you agree to the requisites imposed by the computers or pets that embrace that concept. I'm sure their requirements are considerably less stringent than your classmates.

Sure, your entire academic career should be dedicated to study, learning and scholastically performing. However, it becomes eminently more important that you actively cultivate the perks of social conformity. But wait, to be fully immersed into social conformity, you must first belong. Belonging is that crucial step that propels you beyond mere acceptance. Belonging actually makes you a member of "us," and "we." When you belong you can openly peddle your magnificent mental, physical and coolness qualities as a contribution to the group to which you belong. Those within the group can now embrace the glorious attributes you epitomize.

Unfortunately, you do not yet see that there is a potential dependence on belonging and it can indeed be perilous. Belonging can quickly develop into an aphrodisiac capable of slowly robbing you of certain portions of your sense of self, and possibly even a bit of your self-respect. More importantly, it can stymie the development of your capacity to think and reason independently. If you let it, your group can serve as a comfortable replacement for those tedious acts of personal thinking and decision-making. And those in your group are always willing to counsel you on which decisions are the right ones. Dependency and/or co-dependency is what you can now depend on.

So, in belonging, you get these really great benefits: a support group, an ego-building acceptance group, a source of thoughts and decisions and, most importantly, a higher level of recognition by the really cute one.

Just think, all of this is yours simply because your subconscious dictated that you buy into the pitch: "If I don't conform I won't be accepted. If I'm not accepted, I won't belong. If I never belong, I will be alone. I don't want to be alone, therefore I need to belong." So you ultimately give in. You belong by accepting others who, in the midst of their own fear of rejection crisis, give in by accepting you.

But, deep down inside, you don't really and truly accept them fully. The reality is they don't entirely accept you either. The mutual desire to belong is the true bond, not some unconditional mutual acceptance. The buy-in of the conditional mutual acceptance sales pitch is what's being acknowledged. It's the small print on your non-binding, unwritten belonging agreement.

Your brain excretions soon tend to mimic those of the really super-duper friendlies you have chosen to hang with. But, in your brain's subconscious opinion they're really not that super, instead they're actually mentally less competent than you are. Unfortunately, at this tender age you don't yet realize how incredibly intuitive your brain is, so you don't really listen to it too much.

Regrettably, being driven by the desire to belong, or any other desire for that matter, does, at times, alter your principles just enough for you to, well, let's just say that your instincts to avoid trouble are extremely vulnerable at this age. Just how far you're willing to let this belonging issue drive you depends on how heavily you bought into the "necessity to belong" sales pitch.

From time to time we all barter our principles for our wants and desires, and sometimes even our needs. And a greater desire sometimes requires a greater sacrifice of principles, not to mention the increased susceptibility to even more, desire-fulfilling sales pitches. Getting the things you've been led to believe you should want is addicting. The question will always be: Are you getting what you want primarily by way of your sales pitch skills or by simply forgoing your principles—or maybe a little of both? Any difficulties that you have with either conflicting principles or your desire to belong will soon be compounded many fold by a condition exerting more pressure and influence than purely your cohorts. Stay tuned, you will be satisfied, or hope to be.

When it comes to your friends and classmates, you jumped through all of the "I accept you, you accept me" initiation hoops and made it into the "I belong here group" you wanted. You pitched them, they pitched you, you pitched them back and you both finally bought in. It's time for the real reason you wanted into this group to begin with. You are now free to somewhat confidently pursue the really cute one that you are finally able to converse with. Okay, we are now talking about sales pitching on a significantly higher level. We are talking puberty-based social manipulation here.

That Volatile Mixture of Curiosity and Puberty

Somewhere about this time you develop this bewildering hormone thing that begins to take control of your motivation stimulus directive. I mean, really, could the timing of this self-imposed belonging obligation be any worse? Just wait til you first attempt to engage in a simple conversation with that really cute one. And you seriously thought you were in control of your life.

You may not even be in control of your tongue when you attempt to speak. No worries—it's just a spontaneous conflicted impulse. This impulse is brought on by a dopamine, puberty, anxiety and curiosity cocktail that has temporarily taken over your brain, and usually some other parts of your body as well.

The Agony and the Ecstasy of Social Manipulation

The art of being accepted, liked, and, of course, making out with the really cute one.

It is now fairly important that you develop the skills that will enable you to tactfully and artfully exploit a specific individual. This is, after all, a slightly more important form of manipulation. It actually requires a higher degree of communication skills. Yes, middle school and high school are where verbal communication proficiencies evolve from that of a babbling idiot to that of a slightly more eloquent idiot. You still lack the requisite competence required to verbally express emotions, desires, affections and insults in a way that accurately reflects your intent.

What you really want to say seems to get firmly lodged somewhere in your brain, refusing to come out through your mouth. But that's okay. If others at this age had the ability to accurately and succinctly express themselves, every member of their less eloquent herd would detest them. I recall a girl in my brother's high school class who was just like that. Everyone disliked her, even when they voted her prom queen, student body president and most likely to succeed. Talk about manipulation by communication. Man, did she ever sales pitch every poor little envious student in that school. And really, envy can be such a downer.

The standard and most frequently articulated form of one-on-one sales pitch manipulation is known as the "line." Its renowned effectiveness has made it the primary sales pitch introduction technique for generations. One characteristic of this type of sales pitch is that it begins as an opening gambit. It's really nothing more than an amusing diversion or redirection of attention toward you. The purpose of the "line" is to instantly generate a favorable impression, as well as the requisite desired response. To be successful there are certain compulsory rules that are associated with the content and delivery of these "lines."

When presenting a "line" there is one primary obstacle to overcome. The recipient of this "line" is typically aware of its intended purpose, so in order to be effective the content must be either extremely sincere or intrinsically amusing. The subject or target must also not be repulsed merely by your presence. This condition renders the "line" totally inconsequential, regardless of its moving sentiment and/or enchanting humor. This repulsion also usually results in massive amounts of embarrassment, feelings of inadequacy, and humiliating rejection.

You compose, study, and practice the techniques that will enable you to articulate your lines as if: 1) they are either believable or at least sound like the truth, 2) they are not too lame, and 3) they seem really sincere— you know, *as if you really mean it*. Now none of these lines need to be honest, just sort of. As stated in #3, *"as if you really mean it"* is all that's required

Your powers of persuasion are put to the test here. Your goal is for him/her or the "others" to fall for what will obviously be your enticing and skillful presentation. After all, regardless of sincerity or truth, a "line" is merely a personal little sales pitch you employ in order to get what, or who, you want. You persistently engage yourself in the use of lines because you know when successfully presented, a line can yield new emotional and, possibly, physical rewards. You also realize that unsuccessful lines can drag you to the agony of defeat. This risk/reward ratio enhances your thought process capabilities when confronted with your hormone directives. Strike that. No thought process will ever overpower the dictates of your perpetually demanding hormones.

You learn to ignore your nagging, guilt-tripping inner self pitches that involve pesky mental decisions. Like the ones that involve life-altering transitions from what kind of "line" to lead with to what kind of "life" to lead. These decisions usually result in some form of character development. Of course you stick with the "line" decisions and push the life-directing decisions as far ahead as your procrastination will tolerate. You know you will catch up with them when the eventual "obligation sales pitches" convince you to do so.

Throughout your school career the decisions you make are the predominant factors in determining the extent of your conformist, status-seeking quest for acceptance by that really cute one. Your decisions are the integral parts and pieces that make up your intricate "Social Manipulation Sales Pitch Playbook."

Seeking Comfort Through Discomfort

A little perspective may be helpful here. There are times when people will do what seems to be the strangest things for the strangest reasons. During my college years I took some winters off to be a full-time ski instructor. Teaching people to ski exposed me to some glaring contradictions. A large number of my students were these middle school and high school students. There was a question that repeatedly crept into my mind. Why were all of these kids exposing themselves to miserable, bone-chilling conditions in order to learn the awkward skill of skidding down a frozen hill on two boards while wearing cumbersome bundles of requisite head to toe motion restrictors, i.e., parkas, helmets, goggles, snow pants, ski boots and big fat gloves or mittens? Why on earth would anyone want to do this? I even had to ask myself, what made me want to do this? Could there possibly be comfort to be had from this massive dose of self-imposed discomfort? Obviously the answer is yes.

My time as a ski instructor taught me that people will subject themselves to all manner and degree of discomfort in order to attain just the prospect of comfort. In learning how to ski, however, it's a bit more complex than simply the satisfaction gained from acquiring a new skill. The sales pitch is not that you will learn to ski. The promise is that, once learned, it's fun. More importantly it is the promise of being accepted and admired along with a communal sense of potentially belonging to an envied group of the accomplished experts. Even the inherent risk of broken limbs is not enough to dissuade a first time beginner from this quest to be as proficient and happy as these heroes of winter. Introspectively, I'm sure that was my reason. That and the ever-present possibility of riding up the lift with the really cute one.

Living to Impress

The clothing you buy, the hairstyle you wear, the brand of shoes you strut in and even the personal attributes you brag about are all part of this decision-making process. And every one of these decisions is made with various objectives in mind: to impress, to gain acceptance, affection, companionship, etc. The moment you depart from your front door each morning you embark on a daily mission to sales pitch an image that you, in all probability, copied from those in either your established group, or the group you're trying to be in.

You are not alone in this personal sales pitching quest. From the nerdy geek to the highest ranks of the physically desirable gods and goddesses your school has to offer, the desire to impress is not only a driving force in your social realm, it is also just as influential and compelling to their lives as well.

On one hand, this is a product of human nature. It's akin to a genetic practice field for finding a mate and perpetuating the species. On the other hand, it is the facilitating catalyst of free enterprise. Seriously, where do you think you learned what's suitable, appropriate or personally beneficial to your social acceptance?

Why do you use pimple cream or toothpaste with teeth whitener? Why is the brand of your book-laden backpack or the trademark on your running shoes important? Did some not-so-subtle advertisement subliminally tell you, in all-caps, "THESE ITEMS ARE ESSENTIAL FOR ACCEPTANCE?" Or are you simply trying to fit in through emulation? Why do you so relentlessly attempt to conform to those in your group? Did the same items in the advertisements impress you or are you following in the fashion footsteps of those in your group who previously bought into a media-driven sales pitch? Are you simply a copycat conformist or did you rationally and objectively make your own appearance decisions?

Few, if any, are impervious to "word of mouth" or "identity" conformity. Acceptance is "fitting in" and it is comfortable. If you are that rebel with the courage to present yourself in a fashion contrary to your peers and face the social stigmas and criticisms that accompany such behavior, I applaud you and bow to your superior and unique individualism. This rugged individualism does not, however, preclude you from being susceptible to the abundance of sales pitch assaults you must perpetually endure. Those you choose to be with are either a fundamental reflection of the cool person you want to be like or someone you want to control. And, of course, there is the really cute one, but that's totally dependent on the cute one choosing to acknowledge your existence.

Status

Ah yes, status, the social itch that perpetually needs to be scratched. It is a primary adolescent human objective. As stated previously, status is the distorted window through which the "others" view you, and thus determine your social worth. The quest for status is primarily a product of peer pressure. Thus status eventually becomes the status quo. Driven by this peer pressure, individuals often engage in actions outside of what would be their normal realm of activities. When peers act as a group the activities can sometimes stretch into behavior that exceeds the limits of social acceptance or even the law. The will to avoid rejection or gain acceptance has even provoked a willingness of some adolescents to engage in socially unacceptable, or even illegal activities; i.e., sexting, cyber bullying, etc.

Sexting has become so casual that it has been referred to as modern day flirting. Some are oblivious to the consequences. Others are aware of the ramifications but remain willing to sacrifice personal privacy and face the possible penalties in order to gain the acceptance. And, just as it has been for each new generation, the fabric of moral norms gets stretched just a tad bit farther.

But alas, in spite of the ability to maintain only a small degree of status-seeking self-restraint, most people's self-perceptions become artificially inflated through an illusion of status. In spite of being an ever-elusive objective, status endures as perhaps the single most socially and economically influential force in modern American life.

Returning now to your early education stages, school is where you've been forced into a closed society with people not of your choosing. Your social survival is dependent on interaction with at least some of these people. While some are more successful at interacting, it's a great deal more difficult for most others. I spent most of my academic life in the "more difficult for others" group. While I did interact with a pretty good size chunk of the student population, I distinctly remember my social contact as being very guarded and quite uncomfortable.

Successful social interaction is pretty much "determined by" the opposing dynamics of motivation and risk aversion. True status seekers are those who crave the greatest acceptance. Those who avoid mass acceptance or are shunned by status seekers are generally considered anti-social, rebels, outcasts or misfits. (This is generally where the bullying takes place.) It's a micro version of class warfare and the world's conflicts outside of the campus confines. There are always a very few lucky ones who are naturals. The "cool without even trying to be cool," I refer to this as the "Van Wilder" syndrome.

Now here's the thing, each and every one of these social disciples (students) you've been stuck with in this educational abyss want the same acceptance, status and sense of belonging you do, and possibly more. Some of these greedy jerks actually want some of it from you.

The most aggressive attention seekers relentlessly attempt to transition you from being a sales pitch arrow to being a sales pitch target. You experience an awkward transformation that takes you from being the pitcher to being the pitched. It's no longer all about what you want. You're targeted as a recipient of their persistent intent to manipulate you toward fulfillment of their insignificant, self-centered needs and wants. And they do this with absolutely no regard for your selfish needs.

This is the world of scholastic social competition. They want your attention, and you want theirs. You want to impress them, and they want to impress you. Such is the subtle power of social sales pitches of youth.

"How could they possibly believe that any of them deserve my attention more than I deserve theirs? Man, school is a really screwed up place."

And you haven't even been exposed to the real world yet. Oh how the frustration of youth doth suck.

Unfortunately, there is a potential dark and dangerous downside to acceptance and belonging. There are those who continually build on and reinforce each other's extreme or even deviant behavior. This sometimes results in perilous or negative consequences.

Eric Harris and Dylan Klebold of Columbine infamy are an example of taking a shared reinforcement of an ideology to extremes. Who you choose to hang out with sometimes results in who you "hang" with. It really doesn't matter if you're the dominant leader of your close-knit pack of excitement, pleasure and "justice" seekers, or simply a hanger-on follower. You may get to participate in the consequences no matter your roll in the mischief. Being part of a group often takes you in directions that neither you nor any others in the group would go by themselves. (A little more on this in the "The Herd Mentality" chapter.)

The Academic Powers That Be

Now, while all of this personal and social maneuvering is taking place there are larger factors also attempting to give you a little manipulation nudge. The school itself has an agenda and it keeps a ubiquitous eye on you. Your peripheral mental awareness perceives this as only a subtle backdrop to your vigorous social life. You comply with all the rules in pretty much the same way one obeys traffic signals. While the rules of the road were implemented for everyone's safety, the rules of school exist, theoretically, as the parameters that will keep you on the pathway to a productive and rewarding life. This path is lined with what administrators perceive to be the intrinsic values that will mold you into a positive contributor to civilization. At least that was the sales pitch they gave me.

By the time you reach high school you've probably broken just enough rules that you are pretty much aware of what school policy really is, i.e., don't get caught. But, during the high school years something within these rules begins to change. You're treated a little more like an adult. Well, sort of. They do this while retaining that annoying, ever-present nuance of control. They actually demand you act more like an adult but continue to supervise you as if you're still a child. While this contradiction may appear convoluted, duplicitous, somewhat underhanded or possibly even unscrupulous, it's merely their way of telling you they really don't trust you.

This is one of your first exposures to a form of institutional sales pitch deception. The sales pitch is that their top priority is your best interest. But it's a little more complicated than that, isn't it? You find their interests are really more on the order of maintaining a large degree of control over the behavior of the student herd. This, of course, is in your best interest and will somehow make you a better person. The institutional sales pitch is hidden in the "maintaining a degree of control" part and not the "in your best interest" part. The difference between a self-directed management of what you believe to be your own best interest and the administrative guidance (control) of your behavior is obviously dependent on the intent. Therein lays the rub.

You are to conduct yourself as an adult while they maintain subtle control over you. Your choices are simple. While acting as you believe an adult should, you either rely on your own decisions or you submit to their behavior management and supervision model. Their model is based on subjective dictates that they believe will better serve your developmental interest.

If you are the rebel that I suspect you are, you choose to regulate your own actions and thus bring a degree of risk into the equation. Yes, there are potential consequences for not acquiescing to the subtle manipulations of the powers that be. No one ever said that acting like an adult by making adult decisions isn't without risk. If your decisions purely follow the dictates of school policies, you avoid consequences and reprimands. However, you've also been "kept in line" and avoided risk.

Whenever you are "kept in line" your decision-making capabilities, adult or not, are stifled. You're "kept in line" by the power of an institutional sales pitch deception. Under their watchful and "concerned" eye you're free to go where you want and do what you want. Naturally this is under the conditions that they either know where you are and what you're doing or you have otherwise been given their approval.

This kind of mixed message control is tantamount to spurring a horse while pulling back on the reins. Or, put another way, total independence at the end of a leash.

Think parents, except without the family ties, or the bond, or the love. If this appears to be an elusive freedom wait until you see how this plays when mixed in with your beliefs in the arena of politics, religion and marriage. Being "kept in line" is social conditioning that most people either unwittingly or dutifully and submissively surrender to. I guess it's better than the alternative. Anarchy just seems to be such a chaotic direction.

Finally Getting Out

Ultimately you prevail over the almost overwhelming pressures of endless homework and test taking. You triumph over prom night pimples (even if you don't go), and you revel in your abilities to gain peer acceptance. You have endured all of the trials and tribulations that academic life could possibly impose on you, and you emerge victorious. Not only do you prevail, you even manage to retain a small portion of all that classroom gobbledygook you were there to learn. Most of us emerge successfully, albeit subconsciously resentful of the smart and/or attractive ones who had it so much easier or scored so much higher. (Or is that "scored so much easier and had it so much higher?")

You don your cap and gown and celebrate your immersion into the churning waters of an uncertain future. School may not have taught you to swim in any particular direction but it did provide you with the ability to, at least, tread water. It's a good thing too. In the vast ocean of life you will surely encounter the inescapable sales pitch forces of socially manipulative riptides along with the powerful and sometimes treacherous currents of social, economic, governmental and religious sales pitch seas. No worries, you don't drown, at least not yet.

Note: For all who are at odds with what they perceive as bias, inadequacy or lack of proficiency within our public schools, it must be recognized that not just public but all formal education is actually a form of sales-pitched indoctrination. It is nearly impossible to instill knowledge in young malleable minds without introducing some level of biased communication. In defense of the school system in this country, educators do attempt to indoctrinate students with subject matter even though it is often contaminated with bias. In oppressive countries or regimes, educators attempt to indoctrinate students with bias even though it is often contaminated with subject matter. Sorry, but a more sterile method of imparting knowledge does not exist, not even through the use of disinfected computers. Just like bacteria and viruses, beliefs are spread through all we encounter in life.

Chapter Four
– Oh Grow Up –

Rookie Adulthood
Where intentions and desires encounter reality and responsibility.

Everything up to this point has been confined to a spectrum of limited choices. There have been a plethora of restrictions and parameters that either inhibited or totally restricted the choices you made. Parental guidance, parental guilt, friendship or relationship expectations, institutional parameters and massive doses of peer pressure are just a few of the myriad of constraints that were either dutifully self-imposed or arose from all forms of social expectation.

All of your choices were, for the most part, restricted by boundaries you were led to believe would be the best or most comfortable for your life. Once again, "led to believe" is obviously the big sales pitch part. From here on out the restrictions that have formed the boundaries of these choices and decisions will wane or completely disappear. Your journey as a rookie adult now begins. The sales pitches you will confront and perpetrate now require a more mature perspective, unless, of course, you choose the college option.

The college option offers a general postponement of maturity. Along with this alluring enticement, college ended up being the path I felt parentally and socially obligated to travel. There were a series of liminal and subliminal motivating sales pitches that emanated perpetually over an uncomfortable period of years. They involved one of the most effective of all sales pitches, parental guilt tripping. The remainder of inducing pitches involved peer expectation, potential non-conformist shaming, made-up "self-obligation" and the ever-present fear of not living up to my potential.

Option One: College
–Education's Afterlife Response To A Successful K-12–
Advice from a parent to all college students—there are two things you really never want to hear or unexpectedly encounter while attending college: "You're under arrest," and "I'm pregnant."

When I first left for college, my mother told me that no one in the entire realm of higher education had a better mind than mine. She said that this was because my mind had not been used yet. While this may have been "tongue in cheek," I didn't find out until later that she was absolutely right, at least about the "not been used" part. I also found out that almost everyone else's brains were in pretty much the same condition. But, in my own defense, and in the interest of self-preservation, I seldom revealed the inane products of my brain's inner workings. Because of this I got along relatively well with most other students.

Putting aside, for a moment, the constant bombardment of more sophisticated and alluring manipulation forces that each student must endure, college affords the perfect opportunity to hone even more communication sales pitch skills. You practice convincing your folks that you are excelling in your classes and that all they need to do is send more money. You persuade your classmates to share their research so you can go out drinking. You engage a higher-level vocabulary in your attempts to convince professors that you know more than you really do. They, being experienced educators, know that you're pitching them a bunch of bull, but they buy in whenever they are duly impressed with your sales shtick efforts.

It's all sales pitch fun and games until your junior or senior year. You know, when you actually do have to study and/or learn something. Junior and senior years are also a pretty good time to direct your more serious sales pitch agility toward luring a suitable mate. If you haven't already engaged in this pursuit, there's sure to be an acceptable upper class counterpart who will be attracted by your refined and fully developed sales pitches—uh, um, ur, I mean study habits. These are all pretty much trust-based sales pitches. Your folks and friends buy into them because there is a level of trust. They understand that most of what you are presenting them with is a heap of garbage, but they forgo any rational sifting of this garbage in favor of relying on their trust in you. This is known as "faith." While there is plenty of belief-based faith in the world, family and friend-based faith is usually a little more unconditional. Until that time when you really screw them over they will allow themselves to believe that your sales pitches are well intentioned and, at least partially, based in truth.

You tell everyone, including yourself, that your purpose for attending college is the education and/or the diploma. But in reality it is a relentless pursuit of your subconscious desire to get away to a place where you can go "guilt-free berserk." Even before you begin, both your subconscious and conscious suspect there are fantasies to pursue and tremendous freedoms and benefits you can abuse. There is also the imagined intrigue and mystery that lures you to the ivy walls.

Curiosities such as what it will actually be like to experience the absurdity of being stuffed into a closet-sized dorm room with some loser. This is done to motivate you to tolerate those you would never choose as friends and also to sadistically expose you to your true nature. Another purpose for attending is to definitively discover what exactly is the maximum number of parties that can possibly be attended in your first semester. Yet another is to get away from home so you can find out if they will actually miss you, and vice-versa. Still another is the excitement and anticipation of your exposure to a whole new mass of "others" who don't yet know you well enough to reject you; i.e., potential companionship.

The prospect of a college education is really just a bonus. I will refrain from revealing the experiential source of my credibility on this subject. It's embarrassing enough simply admitting that I have a personal sort of experience-based expertise, and that just involves the parts I can recall. Just remember, wild parties are really just a waste of good brain cells.

If grad school is intended, it is really more of a curse. A prerequisite downer for grad school is that you replace two-thirds of your party time with study time. When you choose a profession that requires grad school, you have given into a warped life aspiration commitment. Relevance is relative. Is grad school just you following in another's footsteps? Did the inspirational forces of a successful mentor, a family member or possibly an encouraging educator motivate you? Or were you simply stirred by a feeling of comfort, reward or security that you witnessed in another who was engaged in a profession that required grad school? Wherever you found this calling there was more than likely a sales pitch somewhere at its source.

Throughout your life you are often passively exposed to people or events that stimulate your curiosities and motivations. If you focus on one of these with continued or increased curiosity and motivation you are engaging yourself in a self-perpetuating comfort fulfillment quest. A self-perpetuating motivation or self-directed comfort pursuit is basically you selling yourself on the comforts of a particular direction or activity. Congratulations, you are engaged in the sometimes misguided but often rewarding activity of self-pitching. ("Self-pitching" is its own chapter.)

Either way, if college is the life you choose then how in the world can you ever lose? Well, that would be because, like they say, you can't win them all. No worries though, in real life you win some and you lose some.

Incidentally, college isn't really the real world. It's just one of the rickety ladders in life's little game of "Chutes and Ladders." It's a game you must play during a time that your raging hormones have been set free to lure you away from your logic and reason sales pitch filters. Talk about a distraction, this is the main reason a lot of students don't graduate in four years. Ironically, this is also one of the reasons they chose to attend college in the first place.

When emerging from this stage of life, most people believe they have completed the majority of their sales pitch conditioning. What a perilously naïve and incorrect assumption they will find this to be. The real, substantive, life-altering, sales pitch stuff has yet to be espoused or imposed.

Option Two: The Street
–Being Thrown to the Wolves and Learning to Live with Them –

Aside from some arbitrary financial benefits of a college education's "professional acceptance" diploma, the cost of college is far too high for a bunch of information that you either don't really need or can obtain for free in the real world.

In the real world, a whole lot of crap comes at you from everywhere: computers, books, TV, radio, movies, newspapers, magazines, Internet, billboards, cell phones, public restroom walls and "the streets." Real "street life" can blast a perpetual overabundance of enticing and biased beliefs at you. This, of course, is all done with the sole intention of selling you something.

65

Unlike the protective cocoon that college life affords, the real world provides a perilous journey brimming with a constant and endless barrage of temptations. These are as much a part of life as breathing, sleeping or being uncomfortable on a blind date.

As you embark on your journey, you begin to faintly hear the seductive siren song that will soon indoctrinate you into the acquisition mode of social acceptance and status; i.e., "you should want, you should need, you should have" as well as the ever popular "keep up with the Joneses." Your quest for social acceptance subtly conditions you to accept, or at least acknowledge, other peoples' opinions "OPOs." These "OPOs," along with most of society's superfluous and manipulative assertions, once again require you to enhance your BS filtration system.

You are no longer the casual observer or occasional object of your schoolmate's juvenile cajoling. You are now a full-blown target. You are exposed and you are vulnerable. Now begins the maturing process that compels you to develop into the definitive twofold dupe that human evolution demands each of us to become: a "believer" and a "consumer."

You are truly on your own now. There's no one to protect you from the "others" or even from yourself. Who are you going trust or believe now? Is it your friends, your relatives, your peers, politicians, Twitter, yourself? What makes you think you can trust or believe anything or anyone? This includes trusting or believing you. Are you the gullible and trusting sort, or are you more of a cynical, always in control, sales pitch deflector? Trust me, either way you are vulnerable.

Because you're out in the real world now, everyone, and I do mean everyone, has something they want you to buy into or, at the very least, hook up with. Sooner or later, you surrender to something, or someone.

Don't feel too bad; all but the most cautious, veteran, street-smart cynics are in the same boat here. There are times when you won't even realize that there's a hunt in progress, let alone that you're the prey. This is because you are human.

Humans are a species that have evolved into genetically susceptible sales pitch victims and, paradoxically, extremely persuasive masters of influence and manipulation. Besides, because you are human, you will always want something. Even if you don't, other humans will always be there to convince you that you do. It's been bred into us ever since Fred Flintstone talked Barney Rubble into joining his bowling league.

How defenseless are we? Even the most intelligent and motivated skeptics cannot always defend themselves against the relentless, perpetual volumes of propaganda and so called truths. Be honest now, have you ever blindly referred to the Internet for "facts" and then been gullible enough to actually believe that what the screen revealed was totally truthful, factual, accurate and unbiased? You do know that you can always double check by going online again. I'm sure the Internet would never present anything other than the truth or the facts. Are you kidding? Why would anyone on earth believe this? Well, it's because humans not only want to believe, they need to believe. Believing is powerful because it counteracts the insecurity brought on by doubt. And perpetual doubting leads to the dark side.

As stated before, we all have, almost from birth, mentally created beliefs that emanate from the parts and pieces of sensory input that are made up of the countless little gems of wisdom, outside opinions, and the glut of other accumulated garbage. You have sorted, accepted, rejected and formulated conclusions based on the entangled mass of neurons crammed with a massive combination of interpreted personal experiences and sales pitches you've previously bought into. And remember, everything that is continuously crammed into your massive mental machine is constantly shifting your critical sales pitch BS filtration paradigm.

You have, to this point, mentally manipulated the results of your personal accumulation of perpetual sales pitches along with sensory input that dates all the way back to your birth. And, because you have been subjected to an entirely different set of sales pitches and input than anyone else, you can now argue with all of the idiots who disagree with you. I might also point out once again that in spite of our differences, you are obviously wrong, and I am completely right. I may not always be completely right but, like most other people, I know I'm never wrong.

An undeniable fact of life is that we all need and we all want. The trouble is, everyone who needs and wants to gain from your needs and wants, knows this. They would all love nothing more than to exploit your needs and your wants, as well as your instinctive need to want. Consequently, a vast number of your life-directing decisions will be the result of some form of negotiation with those who would love to fulfill your needs and wants, obviously for a price. Some will be friendly negotiations with the "others," some will be confrontational conflicts with adversaries, but the toughest will always be the belief and desire-based debates that take place internally. Most will invite you to address a single subconscious question: Who's really doing the pitching and who's really being pitched?

Unfortunately, this question is sometimes overlooked or ignored by your conscious mind. It's not unlike the old poker adage, "If you can't spot the sucker at the table, then you're the sucker." So remember, there are only four possible outcomes to a sale pitch: win-win, win-lose, lose-win and lose-lose. Whether pitching or being pitched, your primary objective should always be to end up on the "win" side of the equation.

You Must Sell to Survive

When it comes to selling and being sold to, formal education is no match for real life street smarts. There is a whole world full of different folks out there, and you will need to learn to employ a lot of new manipulation tactics. The key to manipulation lies in effective communication.

Effective communication is the necessary link that facilitates most successful sales pitches. Without effective communication you couldn't sales pitch a fish into swimming. Your post-academic immersion into the real world is when you really need to sharpen your skills at effectively swaying the thinking of this new set of "others."

These skills are mandatory for job security. It is commonly referred to as justifying a position. If you haven't fully developed your communication skills, you certainly won't prosper out there in our fickle society. And our society is, after all, in desperate need of your well thought-out opinions, judgments and conclusions. There are people out there who are ripe for pitching, and, with diligent communication practice, you are just the one who can convince them.

After successfully honing your sales pitch communication abilities the first and simplest place to start is to find out what they want. It's far easier to sell them what they want than what you want them to have. They will always buy into what they want. When you figure out what that is, you're ahead of the game. The easiest way to get what you want is to give them what they want, or at least what they think they want. It also helps if you truly know your objective. If you can't get a firm grip, or at least find the handle to what you want and not just what you think you want.

Employment is a great example. Just getting a job is selling yourself to get what you think you want. You want to get paid to do something. That something is an activity that you somehow believe will be satisfying. Yet a large percentage of employees aren't only dissatisfied with their jobs but with their career choices. Oftentimes people buy into what they have sales-pitched themselves into believing they want.

Almost all conversation is comprised of opinions or a judgment of facts. Almost all of these opinions and judgments are based on beliefs. Almost all beliefs are based on agreement with or a regurgitation of other people's opinions and judgments that, in turn, are based on their beliefs.

People do more than simply defend these beliefs. Everyone has a desire to be right. Defense of a belief is a form of self-preservation. The successful selling of that belief to another is a form of superiority, dominance or power. This fulfills the primal human objectives of satisfaction and comfort. As for affecting life on the streets, yet another belief is disseminated, and the cycle of ignorance is perpetuated. If it weren't this way, the cycle of belief-based ignorance could not endure and regenerate.

The Companion Search

Job one on the streets is finding a mate, or at least someone you can pretend to mate with. We do this in order to perpetuate the species through a consensual social obligation fulfillment. Just kidding. We do this purely for self-satisfaction, personal gratification and because we don't want to go through life all alone. What an incredible cauldron of sales pitch lines we serve up in order to gain this mutual acceptance of the emotional and physical pleasure of our peers.

After somehow cutting one out from the herd—sorry, I meant, carefully selecting a potentially suitable mate from many qualified candidates—a requisite consensual acceptance courtship ensues. A courtship is a long, drawn out and ongoing mutual ebb and flow of sales pitches. Courtships require both sides to endure a relentless deluge of demands and obligations. It's kind of a reciprocity thing. Both sides wish to deprive the other of the comforts or pleasures that they would be obliged to sacrifice or abandon purely for the other's benefit.

Women would have men believe that they endure a never-ending flow of hollow sales pitches from men. And that those men only wish to gain pleasure by depriving them of other singular pleasures they may be willing to forgo for the man's benefit. (This is where the possession-based objectification "she belongs to me" comes from.)

Men would have women believe there is nothing but an empty life without the comfort and security only a man can provide. Incidentally, most relationships begin by someone accepting another simply because the other accepted them. You liking someone for no other reason than she or he liking you has never really been a substantial basis for a lasting relationship. There simply aren't enough sales pitches involved.

Married...With Children

Marriage is the reciprocal acceptance of desired responses to mutual expectations born of codependent sourced sales pitches. Well, sure, that's on the harshly analytical side, but it's quite true.

There are no effective or credible instruction manuals with realistic sales pitch parameters for these types of mutual obligation attachments. Yet marital bliss propagates perpetually, sometimes. Perhaps it's because most marital sales pitches are bought into long before the pitch is even presented. I assume this is either because girls have always been smarter than guys or because the human need for emotional codependency is a far stronger force than any sales pitch.

"Married with children" is simply the opposing side of the first few chapters. Parents are nothing more than compliant slaves to the subtle sales pitch demands that they trained the child to perpetrate on them.

The parents unwittingly assume a subservient position. They reluctantly do this in order to achieve the goal of raising a healthy, intelligent and successful offspring. Most parents pretty much sabotage this goal by implanting their own opinions, beliefs and personality defects—sorry, I meant traits—into the child's gullible little brain. Oh sure, all parents are well intentioned, but face it, few, if any, offspring make it to puberty without a bunch of character flaws or mental dysfunctions. Trust me, the blame rests with the parents. It's almost as if this is a genetic anomaly common only to the human portion of the animal kingdom.

SECTION TWO
Replacing Reality and Facts with Opinions and Beliefs
{The Paradigms of Sales Pitching}

Chapter Five
– Reality vs. Perceptions / Truth vs. Beliefs –

Reality vs. Perception

Do the distorted carnival and funhouse mirrors reflect poorly on you? Don't fret; it's just your belief-based perceptions being adjusted to the reality that sometimes reality isn't real.

Do you perceive that life sometimes moves at warp speed? Or does life sometimes move at a speed that warps the reality of what you perceive? After all, even the greatest human mind can only gather a finite amount of information at a finite rate in a finite amount of time, without warping.

How do you perceive others? How do you perceive yourself? How do others perceive you? How do all of these perceptions differ and where did all of these perceptions really come from? Now, how close to reality are any of these perceptions? Believe me, they're farther apart than you think. The reality is, reality ain't all it's cracked up to be. At least we never seem to believe it's quite as important as our perceptions.

One of the main problems with perceptions is that they always seem to lock in with such a firm degree of permanence. Because of this, most people's minds are made up before they've learned to rationally analyze the legitimacy of their observations. Believing so often precedes thought.

You may have heard the old parable of the blind men and the elephant. The origin of this parable is disputable, but each variation of the storyline is similar. Most versions are religious in nature, but this story is applicable to human perceptions and the resulting beliefs on many more levels than religion. What follows is an attempt to convey the tale, hopefully in a way that will communicate its intent.

The parable goes something like this: A Rajah, somewhere in India, gathered several blind men together to examine an elephant. The blind men asked, "What is the elephant like?" They were instructed by the Rajah to discover for themselves. Each began to touch the elephant. One by one they began to describe what they felt. The first one, after carefully examining the elephant's leg, described the elephant as being like a pillar. A second man, having only felt its ears, said that it was like a husking basket. Similarly, the man who touched the elephant's tusk said it was like a plough. The others each went on to describe the particular part of the elephant they felt. The head was described as being like a large pot, the body as a granary, the tail as a snake and the tip of the tail as a brush.

In this story, each man had obviously missed the totality of the elephant's true nature. They had each taken their limited perspective to be the total picture. The men then came to blows, fighting to defend their individual ardent belief that what each had experienced was a more accurate version of reality than the others.

The rajah then says in part, "For, quarreling, each to his view they cling. Such folk see only one side of a thing."

Incidentally, both men and women often choose to define the reality and totality of each other by their parts in much the same way as the men in the parable. The point is: that which is observed or perceived often becomes a solidified belief that manifests itself as the total reality of a thing, even if it is only a rear end and not really a brain. So, the result is often that our perceptions leave us vulnerable to all manner of deception. These perception deceptions are yet another effective form of sales pitching. Deceptive sales pitches can, and oftentimes do, manipulate people's actions and behaviors right along with their beliefs.

Most warped beliefs are accepted, embraced and maintained primarily because people's BS filters have been polluted or obstructed (oft times through a good dose of fear). Damaged or fouled BS filters are the conduits through which racism, political bias, religious persecution and other vile human characteristics have been allowed to ooze.

The line of distinction between reality and perception also becomes fuzzy when tangibles or illusions are in direct conflict with perceptions. Like when an adopted child finds out that mom and dad aren't really mom and dad. It can also be when you perceive that the really cute one smiles at you, but suddenly you realize the smile was intended for some perfectly postured, perpetually primped persona in a provocatively posed position just behind you. Events like these can also have a huge subconscious affect on self-image. *(Self-image is just you sales pitching yourself into believing that you really are the person you think you are.)*

On the action side, beliefs driven by sales pitches can initiate, motivate, instigate or perpetuate behavior. Throughout history a countless number of people have fought and died for beliefs that were later determined to be unfounded, misguided or simply irrational. These are beliefs that were bought into and subsequently acted upon. Many have mindlessly, and voluntarily, given their lives for the beliefs of others. Terrorist organizations and rebel factions effectively indoctrinate the young into beliefs so powerful that they voluntarily take their own lives for a sales pitch. Do a few gullible and maliciously misguided Americans signing up for ISIS ring a bell?

Paradoxically, others have been manipulated into voluntarily following orders in situations they had been involuntarily forced into. Nazi death camp prisoners submissively marched, without resistance, in total mass resignation to their deaths in slaughter pits and gas chambers. Had they given into a mutually understood belief that death was eminent and resistance was futile? Had this desperation resulted in a complete resignation of will and a "why fight it" belief? Had they already given up all hope and no longer cared to live or had they been worn down to a state of total mental exhaustion? Either way, forced, inflicted or compulsory beliefs can take the mind to a breaking point. This is perhaps the most extreme example of a forced sales pitch imposing a belief that total helplessness can exist. Brainwashing, solitary confinement and most other methods of torture are forms of forced sales pitches.

There are those who can negate the feelings of helplessness by escaping into their own brain. The mind actually has the ability to mentally isolate and block the recognition of external realities as valid. Oh sure, the agony of torture is real, the anguish of starvation and physical isolation are real but they aren't acknowledged as the central focus of the brain. Rather, they are distractions and interruptions of misery that temporarily disrupt the primary mental focus. So whenever you're in a desperate situation, remind yourself that there is almost always another valid perspective that can be successfully self-pitched internally so as to effectively negate any externally imposed sales pitch or belief, even if it reaches the limits of agony.

The Helsinki syndrome is another manifestation of a coerced belief directive. This is where a captor or kidnap victim begins to sympathize with, identify with or even bond with the captors. The victim forms a dependent or subservient relationship identity that is reliant on the will of the captors.

Truth vs. Belief

Okay, truthfully, what exactly is the truth? The truth is that absolute truths only exist circumstantially. Outside of absolute truth there is only that which we believe to be truth. There are multitudes of believed truths. One type of believed truth is philosophical truth, another is perceived truth and yet another is simple bias or interpretation-based truth (opinion). Truth be told, there is no concrete truth to any of these truths.

This is not to say that when someone points to a car and says, "Look, it's a car," that it isn't a truth. It may very well be a car. But other qualifying circumstances can and often do exist. If someone says, "Look, it's a car," and it's merely a picture of a car, is it really a car? No, it's actually a picture. The introduction of a value judgment like, "Look, it's a beautiful car," takes it even farther from an absolute truth. In a slightly altered context, suppose that the car referenced is actually an old, non-functioning heap that a homeless person uses as a dwelling. In "truth" is it still a car? It certainly isn't to the homeless person. We're talking context, circumstance and perception here.

The illusion that any truth is absolute exists only within the context that it's presented. Outside of contextual parameters, truth is malleable and vulnerable to manipulation, interpretation and deception by sources that are not bound by a specific context. These are the "believe me when I tell you" or "trust me when I say" sales pitch sources.

Truth: $3 + 3 = 6$. This is what we all learned at one time. Within a certain context, it certainly is an arithmetical truth. However, outside of that context it is not necessarily an absolute mathematical truth. This mathematical truth exists only when calculated in the context of base 10. When adding $3 + 3$ in base 4, the corresponding mathematically equivalent sum "truth" is 12.

Truths that lack essential specifics can be twisted, contorted, manipulated and subjected to value judgments purely for the purpose of augmenting a sales pitch. Examples of these "illusions of truths" are often exhibited in cases such as "believer" vs. "non-believer" religious discussions, "right" vs. "left" political disagreements or personal, "My dad can beat up your dad" boasting. And, as is the case with most effective sales pitches, there are always the requisite minute degrees of truth that can be presented to affect desired responses.

Without at least a modicum of truth a sales pitch has little chance of being successful. Even a masterful manipulation of perception or judgment requires at least a seed of credibility. That credibility is based in preconceived interpretations of a truth or opinions aligned with a commonly accepted understanding of a truth. Remember the funhouse mirror. You expect to see a distorted reality of yourself. If the reflection presented a distorted automobile, the image wouldn't contain the requisite modicum of reality. No reality, no credibility and no truth: totally unsuccessful sales pitch. So always remember to include at least a smidgen of reality whenever you're sales pitching the really cute one.

Most deceptive sales pitches rely on a misrepresented truth as at least one of the ingredients. However, in a misleading sales pitch the opposite of truth, in most cases, is not simply a lie. Rather, it's a misdirection, misrepresentation or reinterpretation of a truth that's presented as ambiguous in order to manipulate or persuade.

The skepticism you are feeling about this is merely a result of your time-tested, but biased, "BS" or sales pitch filtration system. The key word there is "biased." Once again, your acceptance of a truth is based on, or biased by, all of the previous "truths" that you "believe" to be truths.

Don't sweat it too much. Everyone's truths are biased by previous truths that were likely gleaned from other prejudiced truths to begin with. I hate to burst your bubble, but Columbus didn't discover America. Native Americans, Vikings and other meandering marauders were traipsing around here long before old Chris did his infamous three-galleon jaunt that eventually landed him in the realm of believed legends. And that, my friend, is yet another in my long list of "truth"-based sales pitches.

It should be pointed out that "truth" and "reality" aren't interchangeable terms. Both are interpretations of what's believed to be true or real, they differ in both the perception and the context of a belief.

Many believe there's power in truth. There is, but there never seems to be as much power in truth as there is in belief. This is especially true when a belief and a truth are resolutely held to be the same. A belief is a personally accepted interpretation of truth or reality. It is most often a biased perception of truth or reality because it's gone through the BS filtration system of a lifelong mental accumulation of judgments. What you believe and why you believe it stems from everything you have mentally processed, refined and regurgitated throughout your entire life.

Beliefs are why people are vulnerable to certain types of sales pitches. Beliefs foster susceptibility to sales pitches that may offer to bring comfort, security, encouragement and self-assurance by simply reinforcing beliefs. What do you think made the pre-technology traveling salvation tent sermons so popular? It would seem that the human thought process has become more indulged in, and dependent on, beliefs than on facts.

Belief reinforcement is one of our favorite pastimes. It provides us with a validation of or our righteous and infallible self-image. That's why we're always right. Well, maybe you are, but certainly not me. I'm never always right, but I'm hardly ever wrong.

We crave, and sometimes even demand, something to believe or believe in. This condition is primarily the result of a lack of skeptical mental attentiveness to our perceptions coupled with a critical scarcity of applied critical analysis. Scrutiny, empirical awareness, reality and fact recognition are skills that a whole lot of people seem to avoid by simply trusting more in their own beliefs and the beliefs of others.

The turmoil proliferating throughout the world appears to indicate that our cumulative ability to decipher truth and reality from subjective opinion and ingrained beliefs is steadily diminishing. It would also seem that our ability to objectively think and reason is diminishing in an amount inversely proportional to our ever-increasing access to "corrupted" or "contaminated" information.

The interjection or application of any form of bias, interpretation, opinion, qualification or judgment into available information, either overtly or implied, renders the information "corrupted" or "contaminated." The incredible lack of skeptical thought process or rational reasoning applied to our ever-expanding access to information exacerbates the illegitimacy and fallacy of its truthfulness, its accuracy and its correlation to reality.

The redistribution of reinterpreted facts and truths further dilutes both their accuracy and credibility. This mitigates credibility exponentially when perpetually disseminated. The eventual result of all of this is that reality is increasingly based on beliefs and beliefs are based less and less on reality. At least that's what my reality allows me to believe and what my beliefs allow me to accept as reality.

Belief Dependence

Why do you believe things to be true? Is it because of your faith, your upbringing, what you've experienced or because of what you've been taught? You do understand that what you've been told or taught is primarily nothing more than what another has experienced or been taught and passed along to you. And, they, in turn, received this perception of reality from the beliefs, perceptions and experience of still others, and so on, and so on.

The percentage of the population that truly believes in superstitions, wives' tales, sorcery, mental telepathy, clairvoyance, miracles and ghosts actually exceeds those who believe in evolution. Their beliefs came from external sources. No one dreamed up these mythical and unsubstantiated beliefs all by themselves. They systematically bought into what was presented to them by "others." From there these superstitions and falsities burrowed their way so far into our belief system that they become an accepted and credible part of our culture.

A simple example of this is the number 13. The number 13 is deemed by many to be unlucky. During an earlier period in our country, many high-rise buildings had no 13th floor listed or indicated because of the inherent "bad luck" risk. To this day there are people who are extra vigilant on Friday the 13th for the same reason. The results of a couple of surveys and a study estimate that somewhere around seventeen million people fear Friday the 13th. If you are one of them, you should probably avoid black cats and breaking mirrors on any Friday the 13th. I'm almost certain that sometime back in our history, the distinction of unlucky was bestowed to the number 13 by the unlucky result of someone's 13th sales pitch.

Some beliefs are the result of a misinterpretation of conveyed beliefs that were ambiguously presented. Believing a misinterpretation is really the buying into a self-deceiving understanding of a sales pitch. This flawed belief is the result of a personal miscommunication that resulted in a flawed interpretation. The classic old personal communication experiment of passing a secret around illustrates the limited accuracy of communication and how it can proliferate into a myriad of flawed beliefs. The experiment involves conveying a message from one person to the next until it makes its way through twenty or thirty participants. The resulting message almost always gets modified, distorted and misconstrued until it bears no semblance to the original message. So, based simply on the pervasive lack of source credibility, why on earth would you believe that anything you've been told or taught is true?

Unverified source credibility is all too often not all that credible. Do you really believe that everything you've been taught is truth or real? The answer is obviously a resounding no. This is because, like most intelligent people, you aren't a totally gullible believer. A breakdown in the reception and interpretation of a communicated belief can ultimately result in a flawed belief. Don't believe it. I certainly don't. When you say, "I can't believe it," there are times when you should really listen to yourself.

It is humanly impossible to deny or even question the validity of everything we have been exposed to. So, to some degree, we have all become dependent on un-validated believing. We must believe because complete skepticism will only get us so far in this world. The same goes for pessimism. That doesn't get us very far either. Most folks are primarily optimistic and are more comfortable wanting to believe. And besides, except for those masochistic delusional philosophers, who would ever want to put out that much effort into being a full-time pessimistic skeptic? Most full-time skeptics are miserable anyway. If they were pessimists as well, they would make themselves even more miserable just by making themselves even more miserable.

If You Doubt It

"I just can't believe it," "I really doubt that" and "Oh come on, that's just not true" are some of the typical platitudes of doubters. They will generally back these up with a predisposition or bias-based selective body of evidence. Just as the believers, the doubters rely on a confirmation bias by seeking out and recognizing only the evidence that confirms only their justification for doubting. Climate change doubters, vaccination detractors, GMO cynics and science deniers have all found just enough self-validating evidence to justify or reinforce their positions of doubt. The source of doubt or disbelief can be the result of contradictory sales pitches clashing with tightly held philosophies and beliefs.

Skepticism, fear, paranoia, or even the stubborn dislike of a source, are all ingredients that can be found in the recipes of a firmly held doubt. Most of the really persistent doubters are not even swayed by facts or definitive research. And, without a doubt, isn't that what true doubting is all about? "I'll never believe anything he says," can be a doubter's sole irrational justification for forming a solidified lifelong disbelief or distrust. A whole lot of conspiracy theories are born of this type of distrust. That's why some people will never vote Republican while others will never vote Democratic, some will never buy Fords while others will never buy Chevys. But one thing can never be doubted: Doubters will always firmly believe in their doubts. I doubt this will ever change.

Do You Believe in You?

We are always told to believe in ourselves. That's a tough one. It would certainly be a lot easier if we didn't know, deep down inside, how incredibly difficult it is to live up to the implied expectations of our own beliefs. Do you believe you are the author of your beliefs, the follower of your beliefs or a victim of your beliefs? I contend that you're a product of everything you've ever experienced through your senses and everything you've been told.

It is also my contention that you have convinced yourself that your beliefs and your interpretations of reality are all pretty much correct. You have also been convinced by others that your beliefs are correct. I say you have convinced yourself primarily because if you constantly doubt your own perceptions and convictions you would either be one of those delusional philosophers, a self-destructive mental case or a pseudo intellectual who would be perpetually mired in your own irrational paradoxes.

Since, and I am assuming here, you are none of those, you accept your own beliefs as valid until you experience a contradiction so compelling that it forces you to amend a belief. This amended belief offers you a new or altered perception of "reality" to cling to. Ah, the comfort of malleable convictions. You see, you have two realities: the reality you perceive and the reality you believe. The closer these are to each other, the more comfortable you are with your convictions.

91

The tangible reality that you perceive around you exists because your five senses tell you there is no way, outside of some whacko philosophical mental games, to deny it exists. Reality doesn't exist simply because you were told it exists. If you can hear it, smell it, feel it, taste it or see it, then it exists. (Except, of course, in the magician's tent. We'll get to that later.) Everything else is something you bought into. An important question here is, did you choose to buy in, were you convinced to buy in, or were you unwittingly manipulated (tricked) to buy in?

You may think that rational thought and intelligent application of mental processes allow you to come up with correct decisions on right and wrong, good and bad, and do or don't. Well, with about ten seconds of deductive reasoning, you will realize that the majority of tools your mind has available to make those "buy into" determinations are based almost entirely on your previously bought into beliefs. These previous beliefs will only reinforce, legitimize, contradict or reject outright a newly presented belief.

As human beings, we use our life experiences and our accumulation of beliefs to determine if a new belief is comfortable or uncomfortable. The comfortable choice almost always wins out over the uncomfortable. The exceptions, of course, are those who choose uncomfortable only because, to them, being masochistically uncomfortable is more comfortable. The bottom line is that beliefs can be ruthless and unyielding slayers of truth, reason, facts and reality. Only truth, reality or a more comfortable or compelling belief can pry loose the tenacious grip of a strong and tightly held belief, that and an intense fear of being wrong.

Can you remember how malleable and susceptible to suggestion our little brains were back in early elementary school? We were almost defenseless against the "power of suggestion." We lacked the analytical tools necessary to scrutinize propositions or advice. An informal, non-scientific experiment conducted back in the 1950s tested the power of suggestion on a class of young elementary school students.

Prior to a simple written test, their teacher casually told the children that studies showed that fair-haired or blond people were smarter and always scored better on tests than dark-haired people. The initial observation was that the fair-haired students sat up straighter and actually appeared a little more confident than the dark-haired students. The dark-haired students slouched a bit and seemed troubled or uneasy. The test was then administered. You guessed it, the fair-haired students scored higher on the test than the dark-haired students.

The following week the children were all informed that the teacher had made a terrible mistake and given them the wrong information. They were then told that the dark-haired people had actually been proven to be smarter and always performed better on tests. Yep, you guessed it again. When a test was given shortly after this revelation, the dark-haired students scored higher and exhibited a happier, more confident appearance than the now melancholy fair-haired students. So here's to all of you incredibly intelligent brunettes out there.

It's Just a Suggestion

Susceptibility to the "power of suggestion" is not limited to the youthful innocents of school children. Might I suggest that this subtle, and sometimes shrewd, form of sales pitch is just as effective on the less trusting and more intelligent among us. Remember the old "pickup line" in the "The Real Cool Fool School Years" back in Chapter Three? These same lines are successfully utilized by, and on, intelligent adults all the time. These "lines" also still employ all of the alluring and compelling flattery that the powers of suggestion avail. And really, who doesn't welcome and appreciate (and totally believe) a little compliment every now and then?

There is a flipside, however. Negative "put-downs" are even more effective. It's easier to impart self-doubt through criticism than to empower by compliment or adulation. The effectiveness of "psyching out" and criticizing opponents exposes a weakness in our fragile human psyche. If this revelation ever applies to you, just give them a big grin and reply, "Absolutely." You'll feel better, and they won't.

The ability to psych out opponents is prevalent in athletic competition. Mohammed Ali successfully utilized poems and axioms as his weapons of choice. Arnold Schwarzenegger, back in his body-building days, would make a competitor self-conscious by pointing out their muscular flaws or shortcomings (even when there were none) in order gain an advantage. Football, baseball and basketball players all "trash talk" opposing players in an attempt to make them feel a little less self-confident. Trash talking is just another psych out sales pitch used to gain an advantage. In poker, a good bluff has the same effect.

Value Judgments

Sure, people absolutely believe what they want to believe. The problem is that people are perpetually exposed to forces that dictate what they should or should not want to believe. The choices are then made to either buy into or not buy into what they are persuaded to believe they want. The catch is, when we are first brought into this world we are subjected to the perceptions and belief systems of others.

As gullible youths we have neither the skills to scrutinize nor the access to viable alternatives to compare these external belief systems to. With no alternate perceptions or beliefs available for comparison, we are all at least somewhat compelled to accept these imposed beliefs as indisputable facts. Having never been introduced to alternative views, how can we accept or reject opinions that we have never been exposed to?

When you are in your vulnerable and impressionable years, why would you question authority figures? For example: when you were very young, who influenced your religious direction? Not until later in life, when you've been exposed to the beliefs of others who championed their own indoctrinations, do you begin a sorting process of what to believe and what not to believe. And, with little or no inconvenience to you, this dynamic process continuously repeats throughout your life. That is, until you completely solidify all of your malleable beliefs.

Desire for a Less Coarse Course

Okay, now that you are armed with your solidified beliefs, you are prepared to venture happily forward in your carefree pursuit of bliss. This is, of course, until you reach either the life-wrenching, or the somewhat liberating, stage of life that is affectionately referred to as "mid-life crisis."

The mid-life crisis stage presents an interesting paradox. You have done what you have convinced yourself you want to do with your life. All of a sudden you find that what you chose was really stupid and not at all what you really wanted. Your old personal sales pitch paradigm has circled around and been ambushed by a self-imposed sales pitch for what you now believe to be your new, true and meaningful life quest. It seems that life's little belief bending and defending is nothing more than a perpetually pending, never-ending bunch of non-offending pretending.

Reality

In reality, reality is merely a sensory perception of reality. What we believe reality to be is, in reality, just a bunch of interpretations and judgments that have been applied to our sensory observations of reality. Another reality is, reality can only exist outside of your brain.

Obviously, if reality existed inside of your brain it would be the size of all reality, and there would only be enough space for one brain. Trust me, there are those who firmly believe their brain fits in this category. It may be that the only things larger than reality are a few egos. A brain can only contain sensory perceptions of reality, regardless of the ego. This is where the reality warp takes place, and thus a warped brain.

You're in a room. The walls, floor and ceiling are white. There's a white door but no windows. A black music box is on the floor in the middle of the room. Incense burns in a vessel sitting on this music box as it plays a familiar tune. When you open your eyes, what do you see? When you touch the music box, what do you feel? When the aroma of incense fills your nostrils, what do you smell? As you listen to the music, what do you hear? The answer to all of these is, ta da, merely the sights, sounds, smell and tastes your brain has interpreted. Is there a music box playing a familiar tune while incense burns on top of it? Let's do a "reality" check. Are there light waves outside of your spectrum of perception? Yes. Are there sound waves outside of the range of your capabilities to hear? Yes. Are there scents that are undetectable by your sense of smell? Yes. See where I'm going with this?

Only the sensory sensations that lie within the realm of the brain's ability to interpret are perceived as reality. If any of the senses are impaired, the interpretation of reality is altered. So which perception of reality is more accurate than another's? Is all of the physical matter that occurs outside of the spectrum of human perception real? Well, it's more of a reality than it is a belief. Even if we can't see, hear, smell, taste or feel it, it exists.

It has been said that a belief only becomes a fact when it has been proven. The meaning of "proven," however, is often held to a less stringent or far more flexible standard than conventional requirements of its definition. In most social, political or religious circumstances the cultural strength behind a belief is often the only requirement necessary to satisfy the factual premise of a "belief." Thus, if it's a universal or mandated belief, it must be fact, i.e., reality. This is obviously to allow "belief" to innocuously slip unchallenged into one's proof/fact paradigm.

This reasoning and somewhat convoluted logic is a deep-seated thought process practiced by the majority of the world's population. Now you know the extent to which a well-developed sales pitch can affect the world. Not to mention the elasticity of definitions. Could this be one of the origins of the world's misunderstandings?

Intent

Sales pitching can bridge the gaps between both reality and perceptions and truth and beliefs. In doing so, they can conceal or mislead through intent. Some sales pitches are based completely on the intent to deceive. This intent is often seeded in greed.

Greed is one of the world's more motivating intents. I'm sure you are aware that many devious sales pitches are specifically designed to deceive, con, trick or unscrupulously cajole a response that will only benefit the pitcher.

Greed has many faces. Most greed-based sales pitches are perpetrated under false pretenses with no intention of fulfilling any of the sales pitch's assurances. Some of the best (i.e., sleazy) con artists can convince even the most ardent skeptics into becoming a dupe or victim of a scam.

The intent to deceive plays to our human inborn desire to believe. It also plays into our desire to pursue comfort and avoid discomfort. If you can be made to believe there's a comfortable reward (generally something for nothing) and all that's required of you is to believe a sales pitch, there's a really good chance you will eventually pay the price. Trust me on this, one way or the other, you will pay the price. Your job as the pitchee is to be vigilant and do your best to scrupulously expose or reveal the deceitful and seductive power of a sinister sales pitcher's intent. Or just ignore it, say no, and walk away. *Wait, don't go, there's still a whole bunch more for you to accept or reject.*

Back in the realm of ordinary, everyday routine sales pitches, the intent is generally a little more benign. If a salesman approaches with a bottle of soda and begins to tell of the wonderful thirst-quenching characteristics of his soda, it is a pretty straightforward sales pitch. His objective, other than the obvious, can cover a myriad of intentions: Just to get rid of it, benevolent assistance to a thirsty stranger, pure monetary profit motive or he's simply had his fill of the other five bottles in the six-pack and this one is left over. Whatever the reason, his general intent is to either help himself, help you, or both. Does the tone of his delivery expose or alter his intent? Does his intent change the sales pitch, or does the sales pitch in any way reveal or disrupt his intent? The answers to all of these speak to the discrepancy between the perception, the truth and the reality.

Depending on the intent, the dynamics of the pitch will alter depending on the responses it elicits. Certain responses may reveal the seller's intent. "I could sure use a drink" will certainly produce a different pitch adjustment than, "Sorry, I'm really not thirsty at all." In this case the intent isn't particularly significant to the process or its outcome.

Intent can have a potentially significant impact or consequence in a slightly different sales pitch paradigm. "You are so incredibly beautiful. I would love to buy you dinner. Would you like to go out with me?" An enticing sales pitch to be sure. It is also a sales pitch with all sorts of potential consequential intentions.

The question of intent is now of paramount importance to the entire dynamic of the sales pitch. This one certainly isn't as simple as getting rid of a can of soda. This is a potential relationship sales pitch. The intent has the possibility of being immensely significant to both parties. There is a vast spectrum of possibilities here. The lives of both party may be meaningfully affected purely by the intent behind the pitch. From a simple pickup line for personal gratification to an emotional and physical attraction that could evolve into a lifelong relationship, both the sales pitch and the response can be life altering.

So, in this worldwide jungle of sales pitches you now have two things to which you can apply your astute analytical skills: the sales pitch itself and the intent behind it. Once you sort out the pitch and the intent you're free to either engage your remarkable decision-making skills or employ your exceptionally well-developed BS filtration system. Remember, it's the intent that differentiates a self-guided directive from a self-justified deception.

It's Just an Opinion

Okay, about now is a good time for another "sales pitch" perspective adjustment, or at least an explanation. What is a "sales pitch" really? It's actually just an attempt to alter, modify, revise or manipulate another's beliefs, opinions or desires. Remember OPOs, "other people's opinions?" Well, it is a collective profusion of OPOs that are responsible for generating the majority of what passes for an individual's cumulative knowledge. Yep, it's mostly OPOs.

People are educated with, exposed to, buy into or are otherwise led to believe what are actually nothing more than opinions. Almost all opinions are usually packaged and presented in a form that we can be readily accepted as valid or factual. Those forms of presentation range from verbal and printed to mass electronic media. From what we all learned in school to what we read in the news or on Twitter, there are very few, if any, actual, adjective-free, unbiased facts. Whatever the source, some OPOs ultimately migrate into our realm of believed reality. No matter how diligent our attempts at disbelief, a large number of opinions never go completely un-believed.

The formal education of most people involves studies in history, social science, physical science, math and the communication skills of reading and writing. Over a relatively short historical period of time, neither the content nor the method of instruction has remained constant or unchanged.

What changed? For one thing, the facts changed. The facts have changed in virtually every subject category. There have even been changes in math. Now if what was presented as fact in the past differs from what is presented as fact today, the old facts were, by definition, not really facts.

If time has altered the old "facts," then wouldn't logic dictate that some of the new "facts" are also suspect and subject to the possibility of future replacement by new "facts?"

Unfortunately, the credibility of any fact also lies in the credibility of its source. In the case of education, the source is totally dependent on their source. When the credibility of a source breaks down, the credibility of the "facts" they espouse is subsequently diminished to little more than questionable beliefs.

Every one of your teachers, professors and mentors believed they were presenting facts. Just because they believed they were facts doesn't make them facts. In many cases, what you actually learned were, in "fact," nothing more than what was believed to be fact.

But hey, didn't that make them facts at the time? Unfortunately, "at the time" has expired and those "facts" are now nothing more than rationalized beliefs that can never again achieve the credibility of factuality. If it wasn't a fact, it wasn't a fact. No take backs. "But what about the facts that were facts back then and are still facts now?" Thank God we have computers that can accurately sort all of that out without any contamination of bias interpretation. *Wink-wink—nudge-nudge, once again with implied sarcasm.*

Now, because you're intelligent, any new belief you accept as valid, and consequently buy into, will miraculously assimilate into your own overall belief system. From there your brain will convert this new belief into its own mentally ingrained truth that you can and will defend as valid. And, when your new personally interpreted "truth" becomes entrenched into your belief system you no longer need to apply your introspective rationality or scrutiny, i.e., you will have no further reason to engage your BS filter.

A really simplified sales pitch flow of logic goes something like this. It begins with the sales pitch (other people's opinions, beliefs or interpretations of either a fact or a reality they want you to learn or buy into):

The subject's sensory input to the subject's brain to conversion by the brain into a perception to judgment (acceptance, rejection or needs further review) of the perception to decision to accept or reject the scrutinized and judged perception (rejection ends the process) to conversion of the accepted perception to a credible opinion to credible opinion integrated in with all previously stored accepted and reinforced opinions to the opinion becomes a justifiable or defensible belief-based, "truth" or "fact." In short, a sales pitch has been believed and totally bought into.

The resulting "belief-based fact" and interpreted "truth" is now yours. You own it. You get to keep and hold onto it until it ferments into your very own mentally solidified pseudo-fact or pseudo-truth. And, since you're not stupid, this fermented and solidified fact can be preserved as more than just an opinionated belief. After all, your belief-based facts have been tested and survived your foolproof analysis, your infallible mental scrutiny and most importantly your good old tried and true BS filter.

This now validated "truth" or "fact" can take its rightful place in your mental "fact-filled" domain. You are now obliged to defend it against anyone who is either completely misguided or too stupid not to have bought into it as you have. So you defend it as representing a factually based reality, a truth or the epitome of absolutism. You defend it right up until an even more compelling or credible opinion-based fact or logic pattern compromises the validity or foundation of your belief. In the event this should ever happen, your sacred belief becomes reduced to a measly little wishy-washy viewpoint. It's too bad you passed it along to your friends. It's your fault they're still going around spewing this opinion-based belief as if it really is a fact.

In a test conducted by a wine company, a large group of wine enthusiasts were brought together for an informal sampling party. They were presented with a red wine and a white wine from the same vintner. The bottles and labels were of the highest quality and design. The guests voiced their conclusive opinions by praising both varieties as being superior wines all during and after the sampling. The guests then participated in a blind tasting with two different red wines. The results were all consistent. Either one or the other was definitely superior to the other. At the end of the party it was revealed that both the red and white wines were, in fact, inexpensive box wines re-bottled into the fancy labeled bottles. It was also revealed that the two red wines in the blind taste test were, in fact, the exact same wines. I guess attempting to impress the herd can ultimately leave an embarrassing taste in your mouth.

Another interesting phenomenon often occurs with group relationships. If acceptance by friends or peers becomes more important than acceptance of a belief, choices often become more complicated. If a belief-based "fact" contradicts a peer group's beliefs it is often easier to choose to go with the group's acceptance. I mean really, isn't rejection by friends more painful than betraying your own beliefs. Personal integrity is oftentimes too heavy a burden to bear in the face of possible rejection. So friendships are kept and another personal belief is hung up in the back closet of compromised principles, along with all of the other temporarily abandoned beliefs. But it's okay because a friend's belief has conveniently and comfortably replaced it.

Incidentally, very smart people are no less susceptible to embracing far-flung ideals than those of us who aren't blessed with rare upper end IQs. They're just more adept at defending them. For example, extremely intelligent people exist at the outermost extremes of both ends of the political spectrum.

Those with abilities to express their side more effectively not only transfer prejudices to others, they reinforce their own beliefs by eloquently refuting opposing positions. This is when a sales pitch and a "self-pitch" occur simultaneously. Because of their formidable communication skill and intellectual prowess, brainy people actually hold onto their beliefs more tightly than the less mentally endowed. No offense to all of you really, really intelligent people, but isn't it great that there's hope for the rest of us?

Chapter Six
– The Primal Forces of Human Nature –
Power, Control, Love, Sex, Fear and Greed
(the motivators that almost sell themselves)

You Know You Want It—Greed and Other Cultural Conditioning

Back when the human race began, need was the primary driving force. Wants hadn't really been fully developed yet. To early humans, food, shelter and protection from the elements weren't "wants," they were "needs." Providing necessities was the essential way of life. As humanity progressed, life became a little more interdependent.

Organized social structures began to emerge. A leadership class developed and gradually morphed into "the bosses," while everyone else was part of the 99 percenters, i.e., the soldiers, the working class or the unemployed. The bosses, those few who were able to secure positions of power and control, eventually became more occupied with indulging their wants. Unfortunately, The 99 percenters, the remainder of the population, were still relegated to a life of struggling to fulfill their needs.

We have obviously evolved a great deal. Leaders are no longer the exclusive pursuers of wants. In more civilized society, greed-for-the-wants has replaced simple need fulfillment as the economic foundation of our existence.

While greed has always been a primal force of nature, the acceleration of the "greed/want" phenomenon within the middle and lower economic classes is relatively recent. As more inclusive forms of government evolved and methods of travel, communication and education advanced, "wants" slowly became more accessible to a greater portion of the population.

Wars and the spoils of war accelerated this process. People began to see the goods, services and lifestyles that other civilizations could provide. This produced, of all things, macro envy, i.e., really big group jealousy. There has always been greed and envy on a small personal scale, e.g., Barney Rubble has a larger saber tooth tiger than Fred, so now Fred wants an even bigger one. Being exposed to new civilizations, however, created a whole new global paradigm of jealousy, envy and greed. More wars and a greater exposure to a whole bunch of new things to want usually resulted in even more wars.

On the defensive "flipside," wars were also utilized to prevent the insatiable "wants" of the "have-nots" from creeping in and confiscating the "wants" of the "haves." Additionally, wars have pretty much been the ideological result of greed for power. Talk about a status symbol of the rich and powerful: "I control more people than you do, so na-na-na-na-na." Childish? Of course, but it does indeed accurately characterize the mutually competitive nature of most power-seeking adversaries.

Whenever mankind had seemingly satisfied basic needs, attentions soon turned to the acquisition of wants. The art of sales pitching facilitated the procurement of these wants quite nicely. The more sales pitching proliferated, the more new wants were created and satisfied. The more the wants were satisfied, the more people wanted, which again, produced more sales pitching.

This acceleration of "wanting" is pretty much what drives the world's economy today. There are even extreme cases where the "wants" are so tremendous they far outpace the number of necessary sales pitches.

This is where the "greed/want" phenomenon evolves into the "just-gotta-have" model. Electronic gadgets and games, big brand cell phones, big brand computers, televisions, digital devices and drones all generate throngs of eager customers, who've self-pitched themselves into waiting in lines in order to fulfill their insatiable need to want.

The quintessential communal talent of our times is that we can, with a simple self-pitch, successfully transform a want into a need, into a need to want, into a "just-gotta-have." Our enhanced digital electronic access to wants has even accelerated our want-based acquisition of enhanced digital electronics.

"Wouldn't you just love to have what they have?" In our modern day culture we are trained to want. It is one of the conditions of living in a free market economy. If you don't want something, you have no incentive to work hard to get it. And one of our great unwritten laws is that if you don't work hard to get what you want, you are a bum and ultimately contribute nothing to society. By contrast, what we generally believe to be primitive cultures that occupy remote areas of the world exist happily by simply cultivating the necessities. I don't believe that even the wisest among us could accurately judge which is better. "Better," in this context, is a value judgment based on beliefs imposed by the respective society. So, depending on which society you grew up in, your "better" may not be better than someone else's "better."

In our society a desire for "better" often brings out our competitive nature. This competitive nature in turn can lead to conflict. When demand for a "better" that's in limited supply, the conflict, coupled with our competitive nature, frequently results in violent encounters.

Most of our competitive nature is manifest in competition for money. Money, being the medium of exchange, can provide most of the "better" we are vying for. This applies to everything from a rivalry for an inner office promotion to a global struggle for territorial control.

The majority of competition lies in a purposeful conquest for personal gratification or enrichment. From early Greek foot races to building multinational corporate empires, or, on the slightly more sinister side, from a backroom game of poker to operating an organized crime syndicate, human competition is universal. Greed and envy are usually the underlying culprits in our inherent competitive nature.

This begs the question, if envy and greed are purely human traits, do they dehumanize us?

Power and Control

With utmost respect for every dictionary out there, I have devoted myself to a long and careful study of the social, political and economic-based definitions of "Power" and "Control." When applied under these cultural parameters, the definitions can be substantively refined, and I have concluded that the more accurate definitions would be:

Power: The ability to deprive, and, to a lesser degree, the ability to enable or facilitate.

Control: The ability to manipulate for a specific purpose through the use of power.

Power

As the fore stated definition indicates, there are a couple of diametrically opposed aspects of power. 1: the ability to enable, and 2: the ability to deprive. An example of enabling would be the general allowance of freedom and liberty that most modern Western civilizations advocate, or, in a more ominous example, lending your car keys to your teenager for the first time.

Historically, however, the ability to deprive, whether explicit or implied, has proven to be far and away the more effective and most often utilized type of power throughout the world, e.g., refusing to let your teenager borrow the keys. Either way, an effective utilization of power will result in the behavioral responses of others.

Authoritarian leaders and regimes have demonstrated that the greater the ability to deprive, the greater the power. (I'm sure this is similar to the parental authority you experienced as a child.) In business or employment, power can be exhibited in many ways. The deprivation is generally understood to be an inherent capability of bosses to deprive subordinates of their individual and collective security. Praise and a raise from management serves to reinforce power through the benevolent recognition of their subservient subordinates.

Historically, benevolent enablement has rarely demonstrated dominance quite as effectively as the ability to threaten people with a deprivation of their security. In the context of "sales pitching," even in our "liberty and freedom"-based society, there are subtle aspects of power that pose a tacit and ever-present threat of deprivation.

Governmentally, these dispositions are generally in the form of subtle coercions or fear mongering that threatens to deprive citizens of security or freedoms. More overtly, impositions such as increased taxes and decreased services pretty much do the trick. Talk about brutal, underhanded sales pitches. In our free market economy, those at the lower end of the economic strata innately feel the threat of deprivation, i.e., survival-based decisions like being forced to choose between medication, food and heating. In most of these cases the true and definitive overriding power lies in the ability to economically and socially manipulate through deprivation and not in a constitutional entitlement of rights.

Whether it's the government, an employer or abusive parents who dish it out to their kids, the powers that be are able to diminish the security and rights of others. The power lies in the "ability to diminish" part and not in the "adherence to the rights" part. This doesn't really concern me, personally, because I am able to maintain the illusion of control that voting in our democratic process affords me, that, along with the delusion that my kids will always do what I want them to. Back when I was a child it all seemed so much easier. I simply threatened to run away…. again. I've tried running away from my kids, but that doesn't really work either.

Now why do you suppose that some people really thrive on this ability to deprive? Perhaps it's the comfort zone of superiority that wielding power creates. Or possibly it's the state of mind that allows them to view themselves as better, stronger and more intelligent. This state of mind also generates a personal sense of security that protects them from feeling subservient or susceptible to deprivation by others. While some thrive on being in a position of power, others find more comfort in remaining subordinate to those who embrace it. It has to be this way, otherwise where would we find the people to have power and control over? In the parking lot, of course. Men are the worst here. Studies have revealed that, generally, when a man gets into his car in a parking lot, he will take longer to pull out of that space if there is another car waiting to fill it. Yes, there is a little desire to control through deprivation lurking somewhere inside of every one of us.

The question here is; What kind of sales pitches does it take to get into these positions of power? Most paths to power involve long-term strategies rather than just a few manipulating sales pitches. Yes, sudden acquisition of power can be realized through violence, brutality and threats of immediate deprivation. This is sales pitching through vile intimidation. Suffice it to say, the abrupt forms of instant power are violent and generally criminal in nature. The majority of power acquisition strategies consist of a planned out series of directionally focused and, typically, ego-driven sales pitches. As it pertains to our society, there are several types of power:

Emergent: *Growing acceptance of, or reliance on, an individual's ideology or actions rather than an individual's attempt, or even a desire, to obtain power. This type of power is inherently inborn or intrinsic rather than attained through motivating factors.*

Position or **legitimate**: *Recognized as legitimate power only when the authority is accepted in the positions they hold.*

People accept this power because they believe it's desirable and necessary to maintain order and discipline in groups, organizations or society. Parents, supervisors, managers, law enforcement officers, teachers, etc. have this "position" or "legitimate" power.

Character: Those who do what they say and say what they mean epitomize this type of power. They exude the honest and trustworthy qualities that compel people to follow.

Coercive/reward: This is an ability to appropriate a subordinate's control over his or her own situation, position or condition. The coercive power is on the punishment side and ranges from a parent's imposed restrictions to a tyrannical government's torture. The reward side ranges from a pat on the head to an appointment to a cabinet position.

Charismatic or **personality**: The ability to intrinsically elicit admiration, esteem, respect or adoration from others. It's based in an air of confidence and personal magnetism that attracts and holds cohorts to loyalty. It's a self-imposed emotional bond felt by admiring followers toward a leader.

Elected or **bestowed**: The demonstration of leadership qualities that result in ability to achieve commonly accepted goals. This power also lies in an ability to negotiate reciprocities and is gained pretty much by successfully employing the same strategic abilities.

Expert or **Knowledgeable**: This is credibility based. Basically the authority comes from knowing more than others.

Bought and paid for: If I revealed what this is, I'd have to charge you far more than I'm sure you'd be willing to pay.

In order to become powerful you must employ one or more of these characteristics of power by "sales pitching" others into believing you are a leader they should follow. Each of these is a distinctive form of power that requires its own respective blend of sales pitch tactics or strategies to attain. Some may involve sales pitches that are implicit, others necessitate more overt or explicit pitches and some involve elements of both. Either way, the ability to persuade, manipulate, obligate or dissuade are some of the most effective skills a truly powerful leader can possess. This is, of course, other than a leader's obvious ability to inflict direct or indirect threats of deprivation.

Every position of power brings with it an exposure to potential corruption. One characteristic that all positions of power share is exemplified by the old, historically verified adage that power corrupts and that absolute power corrupts absolutely. To some degree this saying also applies to one's ability to sales pitch. The more skillful one is at sales pitching, the greater the ability to utilize the talent for unscrupulous or deceitful purposes.

Successful con artists are some of the best sales pitch artists in the world. I'm pretty sure the same can be said for presidential candidates in an election year and teenagers who have just gotten their driver's license. Don't shake your head, no. If you were a "driving" teen once, you know what I'm talking about. These sales pitches were known as the "driving forces" behind the deceptive power over parental control.

Control

Employing power to a specific purpose is "control." There can be no control without the requisite enablement that only the existence of power can provide. Without the simple power required to direct muscle movement, even the control of your television remote is lost. And without the ability to control a TV remote, many people are rendered totally out of control.

Without the power inherent in their rank, generals have no real control over their armies. Control is really just an integrally commanding sales pitch threat backed by an even more imposing power sales pitch. Whenever there is control, rest assured there is some form of power behind it.

Bluffing in a game of poker is a perfect illustration of a sales pitch that attempts to exhibit power over another player and thus control the hand. When control is resisted, the power behind it is tested. When you bluff and lose, you may have lost the hand but presented your opponents with the possibility of future deceptive power. You have instilled a degree of control over their ability to decipher what you conceal. It's kind of like a child attempting to put one over on the folks. I say this just in case you don't quite remember your childhood. Everyone knows you did it, you just hadn't fully developed your ability to successfully bluff your way out of it.

Self-"control" is a different type of focused power. Yes, it often requires some form of personal deprivation in order to be successful: mostly the desire to vehemently express anger or frustration when tact is more advisable. Maintaining control over yourself is sometimes the ultimate test of your power. It takes a powerful sales pitch to convince yourself that you must maintain control.

Sometimes an internal competition for power and control develops. A lot of people seem to lose this competition. Often in life, the sales pitches from outside forces of power attempt to usurp your natural desire for self-empowered control. Political offices, corporate boardrooms and prisons are filled with those who vigorously resisted those forces.

Who or what is in control of you and who or what do you have control over? By now you have probably figured out that you are on the short end of the balance scale on this one. Most people are living life more as objects of control rather than controllers and find it challenging just to control their own.

We all can be deprived of many things: material objects, affection, employment, freedom, loved ones, even life itself. Yes, we all have something to lose. Those with the ability to deprive you of what you have (or even your ability to obtain what you want to have) have power over you. Those who have the ability to convince you that they can provide you with what you want or need also have power over you with their ability to withhold what they can provide. The only power we have at this point is to say "no." This is your only ability to deprive them of their power over you.

The relevance to sadism and masochism won't be covered, except as illustrated by this power and control relationship: The masochist said to the sadist, "Hurt me. Hurt me." The sadist looked deep into the masochist's yearning eyes and, with a cruel and self-satisfying Cheshire grin, replied very slowly, "No." Both the masochist and the sadist revel in their power to elicit the results that provides each with exactly what they desire. There's nothing quite like a good old dose of deprivation to bring out the pleasure and satisfaction of both. Wouldn't you agree? You probably do if you're a sadist or a masochist.

Sex, the Shrewd Method of Selling Yourself

If somehow, you're not already aware: Sex sells. Not only does sex sell, it's actually its own best sales pitch. Almost everyone is enticed by, preoccupied with or, at a minimum, somewhat interested in sex. It meets all requirements of a perfect selling machine. It's provocative and has a perpetual and energetic built-in demand association. It's certainly a mental aphrodisiac. During the adolescent period, it occupies a portion—a large portion, no, no, a massive portion, all right, all right, almost all—of the adolescent brain's activity. It's quite likely the primary curiosity of puberty and prepubescent years. It's often been said, if only by me: "The sex drive is a joyride that provides the best mental scenery." Other than fear and survival instincts, sex is the most effective sales pitch tool known to man. If you can associate sex with whatever it is you're selling, you will, at the very least, have the attention of your audience.

Sex also has its less tantalizing side. Sexual attitudes can morph into the antithesis of the relationship between "sex" and human nature. Shame, embarrassment, inferiority, insecurity, taboo, inadequacy and even criminality are all manifestations of many negative effects or socially imposed aspects of divergent "sex"-generated attitudes. Simple adequacy issues can quickly neutralize the desires described in the Freud's sex drive theory, where sex is the major driving force in human nature. Erectile dysfunction is responsible for some of the more colorful and suggestive sales pitch ads that appear on television. Of course these ads will only run "when the time is right."

Members of every society on earth can relate to sex. I'm obviously referring to the societies that didn't become extinct. Almost everything in our world is somehow driven by sex, or, as those in their puberty years would suggest, driven crazy by sex.

There are numerous forms of sexual display and expression utilized to allure. Fashion, whether subtle or overt, is where almost everything associated with the clothes we wear carries at least an undertone of sexual attraction, or in the case of burkas, sexual aversion.

When it comes to transportation, automobiles are certainly designed to portray sexual allure, especially in their ads. Even minivan interiors are designed to convey sexiness. As for shelter, homes are often designed and decorated to either depict a virile or a feminine comfort and for a reason. Some exotic home designs have even been implemented in a way that suggests evocative cohabitation.

From perfume to deodorant to suntan lotion, people have always utilized fragrance for the purpose of sexual attraction. And even food, yes, even the appearance, aroma, and taste of food can be used to sexually allure. Aren't you kind of attracted by someone who's actually willing to cook for you?

Almost every aspect of our lives has been or can be used as a subtle sexual innuendo sales pitch. What, you've never seen a sexy dress or shirt, a sexy car, a sexy bedroom, or smelled a sexy fragrance or tasted a sexy, melt-in-your-mouth chocolate confection? If you haven't, you're leading a dreadfully sheltered or incredibly dull life. Get out and meet some people. Seriously, I mean right this minute. If you don't, it's a terrible waste of your life's time, not to mention, an awful shame.

Speaking of Shame

As far as sales pitches go, shame can be as powerful as it is uncomfortable. Shame is mostly a self-imposed guilt form of "self pitch," i.e., a sales pitch you pitch to yourself. It normally results from not fulfilling standards, norms or expectations imposed by others. It's not unlike guilt tripping yourself for doing something you know you shouldn't have done. Most of us learn this one early on. It's a tough one to shake.

To partially eliminate its effects you must cease caring about what others think about you and your actions. If you ignore all feelings of inadequacy, obligation, expectations and social clumsiness, you won't feel the embarrassment, guilt or rejection that are requisites in feeling shame. No guilt, no shame. The problem with shame is that it's personal. It's even tougher when you offend someone you really care about. Sure, it's a shame, but you'll get over it (*unless it involves sex*).

Lust for Love or Love of Lust

What does love have to do with sales pitches? Well, pretty much everything. Being either a reason for or a direct result of the aforementioned "sex," love yields relatively the same sales pitch impact but to a lesser degree. Simply put, a sales pitch is how love begins, how it progresses and even how it sometimes ends.

Without a sales pitch, how would anyone find love? Without a quest for love, procreation-based sex itself would be compromised with horrifying consequences. Bars would close down, nightclubs would go broke, restaurants would go under and humanity would cease to exist. The world would become void of the locations where all sex-based sales pitches are initiated and propagated. All of mankind would simply wander aimlessly amid the ruins of a loveless and lustless existence. Oh what inhumanity that would yield.

Two guys walk into a bar. Seriously. Two guys walk into a bar. Why in the world would they do that? Maybe it's because they want a drink. Really? Don't be ridiculous. It's because there might be girls inside. Now why would there be girls at a bar? Because they know that, eventually, two guys walk into a bar.

Is true love really true love, or is it simply an emotional commitment to a mutual attraction of codependent comfort sharing? Is it an intense, passionate infatuation or hormone-driven desire? Is love simply one person liking and totally accepting another person, because the other person likes and totally accepts them? Is it a chemical-based sensory attraction? Well, it's kind of all of these.

Whether it's a true emotional connection, comfortable codependency, chemical cohesion, sexual satisfaction, self-gratification, outward benevolence, real or imagined, love is ultimately a bonding relationship that provides comfort. In other words, it's whatever you want it to be as long, as it delivers comfort. But is it the same type of comfort your chosen mate or significant other believes it to be? Comfort assumes many forms. Security, companionship, dominance/submission, codependency are just a few examples of the many types of comfort people believe love provides. Unfortunately, some find that their beliefs don't always match their mate's. Irrational blind optimism, fairytale expectations, imaginary delusion and plain old wishful thinking are just a few reasons why the commitments required to maintain a lasting relationship eventually falter.

How does a sales pitch fit into all of this? Well, have you ever heard of two complete strangers instantaneously becoming completely and unequivocally involved in an unconditional relationship? Unless the stars are perfectly aligned, the earth rumbles or the laws of probability are shattered, the answer is most likely No. Why not? It could be that relationships require a period of reciprocal knowledge acquisition.

Back in the olden days they called this period "courtship." The more progressive version is the abundantly more suggestive, "hooking up." One of the few real requirements of courtship is that some form of communication must exist. This communication is where the sales pitch resides. Initially, it is a sales pitch presentation of either one's incredible attributes or an overt demonstration of one's ability to provide.

This sales pitch communication can be presented in various forms. It can be verbal banter. It can be physical gesture. It can be perfume, makeup, deodorant, stylish attire or a fancy car. Whether the initial catalyst is a "line," a wink, a fragrance or apparel choice utilized for the purpose of attraction, it's a focused sales pitch with a specific purpose.

It's a sales pitch of seduction that dates to the beginning of mankind. The only sales pitch that may be older is when one man talked another man into lending him a club so he could bop the really cute one over the head and drag her by her hair back to his bachelor cave.

Well, okay, I guess things haven't really changed that much, except that now we go to clubs instead of using clubs.

Fear, Fear, Fear or "How to Rule the World: 101"

Sex aside, fear isn't only the definitive tool of power, it's the gateway drug to manipulation and control over entire civilizations. What exactly is it that produces, creates or generates fear? Where does it come from? How is it instilled?

Like power, fear resides in the ability to implement threats or conditions of deprivation. When others maintain an ability to deprive people of possessions, health, loved ones, freedom, security, life, etc., it has a tendency to make these people more than just a little uncomfortable. When threatened with the loss of any of these, don't we all become extremely anxious and fearful? It's human nature. People are afraid when subjected to a lack of control over any part of their life's situations, but this is only to a certain point. An over-exposure to fear-producing conditions results in fear fatigue. Fear fatigue is where the mind gives into believing that "all hope is lost."

Fear, used as a threat of deprivation, has been, by a huge margin, the most utilized and most effective form of control over other human beings. This ability to deprive that defines power has, throughout history, allowed entire populations to be manipulated for the purpose or pleasure of a few. The simple threat of deprivation is, perhaps, the primary sources of mankind's angst.

To a lesser degree, fear can manifest itself as a phobia. There are tons of phobias, and they're all very real to those who suffer from them. Is a phobia a learned reaction to experiential trauma or a result of inherent biologically sourced mis-perceptions? The answer to both is yes. Drugs can also produce phobias, but since this type of fear has no basis in sales pitches, I'll leave this to the medical experts. (And I'm sure this will relieve you of any fear you have that this particular subject will continue.)

The Other Emotions, You Know, the Real Ones

Most of what we feel, before our brain has the opportunity to interfere, is just about the only process we engage in that isn't completely born of a sales pitch. For instance, pain born of sorrow or loss. This pain is not the emotion we experience just because we feel bad, but rather the true inner sensation of agony. The sudden loss, of whatever is closest and dearest in our life, draws out true sorrow. Nothing we receive through our five senses instructs our brain to create the crushing emptiness we feel deep in our chest. Rejection and failure often produce similar pain, though likely to a lesser degree. The euphoria of love is another. Not so much the love we convince ourselves of when we "fall in love," rather the type of love we experience when our children are born or when a fiftieth anniversary rolls around and we realize that real love isn't at all what we believed it to be fifty years ago. How we each feel and react to these and other naturally occurring raw emotions before the thought process intervenes is more a product of heredity and our inner heart than the imposed definitions, directives or expectations of others. A social expectation "sales pitch" of how we are supposed to feel is often in conflict with what we actually feel.

Internal Driving Forces

Fear of failure vs. drive to succeed, vile distaste of losing vs. intense desire to win, we all have some mishmash of these diametrically opposed components influencing our decision-making.

People do things and lead their lives a certain way for a reason. People either want something or want to avoid something. As stated before, they want something in order to gain comfort or they want to avoid something in order to avert pain or discomfort. People will either succeed or fail to achieve attainment of comfort and avoidance of pain. Success and failure are part of everyone's life. We first experience them both in a sales pitch context shortly after birth. When we get the boob, we've succeeded. When our bedtime cries are ignored, we've failed. From there we begin to develop motivational patterns.

Even though most people like to win and dislike losing, to a varying degree, we all eventually accept winning and losing as part of life. We accept the successes and failures with differing levels of comfort or acceptance. We begin to favor one more than the other. This soon manifests itself into either a comfort-based desire to succeed or a discomfort-based desire to avoid failure. The more competitive among us escalate the intensity of these desires to a higher level of significance.

Interviews with successful athletes and successful business people reveal a distinct compulsion for one over the other. An intense desire to avoid failing or losing drives the behavior of some, while an equally intense desire to win or succeed drives others. Both of these life-directing forces are born of experiential-based beliefs that have been internalized as necessary survival skills. Both success and failure can be extremely powerful motivating factors in any self-pitch-based belief paradigm.

So, win or lose, most of us have a subtle subconscious proclivity to both fail at succeeding and succeed at failing, in spite of our inherent desire to ultimately succeed.

Chapter Seven
– The Herd Mentality –

That Good Old Need to Belong

I'm sure "Yoda" would agree that the dominant influence a group dynamic has on an individual is strong with the herd.

By "herd," I'm actually referring to any type of group that is made up of human beings. The herd mentality is actually one of the primal forces of nature that wasn't addressed in the previous chapter. The "herd" relates more to a macro-cultural framework than it does to a micro or personal level of belief-based sales pitching. Because these sales pitches exist on such a massive scale, I felt obliged to deal with the herd mentality separately.

There are indeed many mighty forces within a herd, particularly within a society-based herd. When deprived of the safety net of a group, most individuals have feelings of insecurity. Most groups, tribes and societies require a delicate codependency. Obviously it would be difficult for a herd to successfully exist without the participation of a few individuals, and historically, individuals rarely survive well outside of a herd. The basic need to survive is at the root of our primitive tribal "herd" nature.

That's right folks, belonging to a "herd" saves lives. Unfortunately, conflicts with competing herds, particularly herds with incompatible beliefs, can take a toll on human lives. Ultimately, it's the promise of security that lures most to seek membership in society-based herds. At least that's what I've heard from my herd.

Okay, simple individual recognition by the herd can also be a huge motivator. The contrivance utilized to gain recognition and acceptance is, of course, the sales pitch. When a deed is done purely for the recognition that it will provide, that recognition becomes both a catalyst and a goal. It is this quest for recognition that drives a desire for acceptance as an individual. This requires that the herd actually acknowledge an individual member's existence.

Unfortunately, most herds only recognize individuals for their screw-ups. When you do something you think is special, outstanding or inspirational, who gives you that satisfying pat on the back? How about criticism? Criticism is praise's nasty sibling. Both adulation and criticism are merely judgments of how well you are complying with the standards that have been set by the herd. It's nothing more than their little sales pitch prompt that enables them to maintain an individual's conformity to the herd.

We human beings have a remarkable proclivity to shield both our beliefs and our perceptions in a protective fog of self-deception, especially at fairly critical times. We know others have a tendency to define us by our beliefs or what they perceive our beliefs to be. How others perceive us can be, in certain instances, more important to us than our beliefs. If confronted with a conflicting ideology during an employment interview, does landing the job become more important than maintaining adherence to a belief?

Believe me, it does if you're hungry or having a tough time supporting your loved ones. This also applies to commonly held herd beliefs. Take for example those zany, madcap, old-world, "flat earth" believers. When scientists of the time postulated, or even demonstrated, the earth was round, they were branded as heretics. Going against commonly held beliefs of the herd has never been a safe and secure route, even when reality rudely intrudes.

Throughout history every society has been its own distinct heard. Conflicts between herds have always existed. It has always been and will always be a battle of us against them: cowboys vs. Indians, our turf vs. their turf, race against race, Christians against Muslims, US against Russia, the Federation vs. Klingons, etc.

Herds are really nothing more than a collective sales pitch that allows, requires, hinges or depends on affiliation or participation. There has always been more strength and security in groups, i.e., the larger the group, the greater the strength, and the greater the strength, the greater the security. The characteristics of a herd are similar to the characteristics of gravity. The larger the herd, the greater its gravitational pull, and thus, the larger the number of additional people it can suck in. And no, I'm not implying that really large herds suck, but larger herds have certainly been known to take control of smaller herds.

Early civilized man quickly learned how much power there is in numbers. People want and need security. As stated before, the larger the herd, the more secure its members. Mankind still depends on the security and codependency of like-minded individuals who are bound by a common need or purpose. The sales pitch here isn't subtle: either survive with the herd, die alone or choose what's behind door number three and spend the rest of your herdless and insecure life lounging in your new "price is right" living room set.

A Unified Buying In, And Its Unifying Effect

For any sales pitch to be effective there must be someone who buys into it. But what if a sales pitch is good enough to get everyone to buy in? You know, when entire groups of people collectively and concurrently buy into a single sales pitch. It doesn't even matter if it's consciously or unconsciously bought into. It still results in the formation or perpetuation of a herd. Sometimes everyone buys in for the common good of the herd's own members. Other times it's more of a conformity thing. A trend, fad, cause, movement or any other mutually accepted philosophical premise, can draw people together like a giant magnet attracting paperclips.

These groups sometimes take on the characteristics of a leaderless flock of blackbirds. Some groups form around a central character or ideology. The key to the herd is the relationship between the individual and the herd and the sales pitch that they mutually agree to buy into. The individual receives a sense of acceptance, belonging, companionship and/or security that only a herd can provide. The herd receives additional credibility, reinforced ideological validation and a fortified representation that only a unified membership or population can provide.

A herd can be as small as a Jamaican bobsled team or as large as a world cause. It can be as leaderless as a uniformly accepted fashion trend or it can be as organized as a political party. Just kidding, it can obviously be much more organized than a political party. The Grateful Dead rock band was the central attracting force behind a massive nationwide herd. Some in the marauding portion of that herd actually believed they were part of the band. Kind of like a sheep believing it's a shepherd. This was, no doubt, less of a dependence on the herd than on the drugs. Such is the strength of the human desire to belong.

The herd mentality means belonging. It is part of our nature. We are all part of one herd or another. Conversely, we often adopt a position of joint ownership of the herd. We boast when "our" college or "our" professional sports team wins. What do you mean "our" team? We may be fans but these aren't our teams. We may be proud of the city or state in which we live, but hey, it isn't really our city or our state.

Over a very long period of time this imaginary supposition of ownership has become embedded in our collective colloquial social culture. This "herd membership" is a fascinating type of sales pitch because so many people buy into it. "That's my team out there" is simply acknowledgment of membership in the herd of fans who identify with that team, unless, of course, you are actually the owner of that particular team. If so, then I am definitely a fan of yours.

From Adolph Hitler's "Aryan race" in Nazi Germany to Jim Jones' "Drink the Cool aid" social imprisonment in Jonestown, there have been many herds of followers who have bought into a single person's compellingly persuasive or entirely convincing sales pitch. Was this because the members within these herds of followers were each lacking personal direction? Or was it perhaps because the leader's sales pitch was so compelling that the followers flocked like children to the pipers flute? It's more likely they bought into the group's sales pitch, because it promised a greater degree of comfort, security or life fulfillment they didn't believe they could provide for themselves.

The seductive attractiveness of the herd can be a powerful and mesmerizing force. This reveals the herd to be a borderless assemblage of unity that serves extremely well as a support group for commonly held desires or beliefs. Once again, does the acronym ISIS ring a bell? The bell it's ringing is the same as the ones ringing in every steeple and bell tower on earth. The followers are often the impressionable or gullible believers who are vulnerable to a comforting promise of self-importance.

Do You Really Belong Here?

"Follow 'us,'" "become one of "us" and "believe as we do"—or you won't really belong. Another downside of not being a member of a group is credibility. If you don't belong, then you are wrong. This is a typical subliminal mass mantra of the herd members. This mantra is merely a reverberation of the siren call of those who actually lead most of the agenda-driven herds. An example of an agenda-driven herd is ISIS. Individuals are enticed by the prospects of contributing to a greater cause. They are united under delusions of righteousness perpetrated by alluring sales pitches.

These sales pitches usually offer promises of personal fulfillment or purposefulness. In reality, participation in a group cause can merely help to facilitate the illusions of the megalomaniacal power-centric pseudo-righteous leaders of the cause. The mantra of these types of herds often defines the parameters that each member must be willing to comply with. Consequences are generally harsh for those who attempt to abandon the herd or the cause. Fear of retribution is what maintains control over the herd. When all of the membership conditions become solidified, the indoctrination (brainwashing) process is complete. And so, from a simple, individually delivered, ideological, promise-filled mixture of sales pitches, an entire army can be created.

Many people seek out groups in hopes of finding comfort and acceptance. Causes, ideologies and religions are herds that people most often pursue to satisfy

135

personal principles or share moral values. Some who seek esoteric or ethereal answers to nebulous questions often feel that comforting remedies may reside within certain groups. In that vein, cults sometimes offer the same type of welcoming comfort as religions or governments.

Now, just because you want to belong doesn't guarantee acceptance into a herd. Some of the more exclusive herds may require proof of your worthiness. Fraternities and sororities are examples of selective types of herds. Status is the element that personifies the exclusivity of these tribal "scholars." A vetting process of some sort is usually employed to verify the worthiness or acceptability of a potential "wannabe" member. In the case of fraternities, hazing is the traditional contrivance that provides proof of worthiness. That, along with requisite good looks, wealth and/or the ubiquitous cool factor. I understand that in some terrorist organizations, one is either accepted or beheaded, regardless of coolness or good looks. I guess some herds are better than others for keeping a-head in life.

The In-credible "They"

Ah, the ubiquitous "they." Now exactly who are "they" and what are their motives? Is their argument, their logic or their authority structured to eliminate questioning, or objection? Is the generally accepted position of "they" above reproach? Is the burden of self-direction and decision-making really lifted if you follow the parameters that the authoritarian "they" would have you follow?

Is it so much easier and so much more comfortable to just go along with and believe what you are told? After all, if it turns out to be incorrect or inaccurate, "they" are the authority, not you. No, you would simply be the fool who fell for it. Or, at least, that's what "they" told me.

How's this for an evolutionary phenomenon? Historically, "they" have had a dramatic affect on social change. Imagine a scientific broadcast news release: "Based on information regarding what we believe to be the facts, we, the informed body of fact interpreters, have determined that you need to change your old beliefs into these new beliefs that we believe are the beliefs that should now be believed."

Now, if "they," The Informed Body of Fact Interpreters, say that it's so, it must be so. Why? Well, it's because they are mankind's unofficial absolute ubiquitous authority. "They" are the quintessential "powers that be" in the collective field of knowledge. This is the sales pitch power of the "powers that be," or at least that's what "they" say. Even the most ardent skeptics sometimes buy into this nebulous source. It's a matter of convenience. "You know what they say," became a platitude for a reason. "They" is just a convenient sales pitch of false or un-vetted credibility.

Institutional Credibility

Do you have a debit-card? This is a piece of plastic that gives you the power to instantly pay money directly from your bank account. Did the public demand this concept?

Was this deemed a service that the consumers of America craved, lobbied for and couldn't live without? No, this was a pretense dreamed up by a few bankers who pitched it to us as a convenient alternative to credit cards.

Please excuse me for a moment while I attempt to sort out the logic. If you make a purchase with a credit card you have a certain period of time to pay the credit card company all or a portion of your balance, with an additional interest charge for partial payment. If you don't pay anything within that period of time, you will be charged the interest and a late fee. It's just like a loan. Either way, you have a choice. You get bills and statements that tell you how much you owe and when to pay.

A debit card, on the other hand, works out really well for the banks and maybe not so well for you. Your money is gone right at the time of purchase. The seller has the money right then. The bank has the records right then. Unless you are one of the few who keep meticulous and timely records on a per charge basis, you won't really know what your balance is until the end of the month when you get your statement. Oops, maybe not so convenient after all, especially if you unwittingly overdraw with an occasional impulse purchase. Whoopee, here come the fees, fees and more fees. Lest you know your exact balance at all times, how is this beneficial for anyone other than the banks and the retailers?

The reason the banks sold this to an undemanding public is because it benefits the banks. Banks actually make more money from overdraft fees than they do from interest fees. Now that's what I call a major monetary incentive—for the banks. The sales pitch they gave us was so good that people actually believed, and still do, that this is a convenient and efficient way for consumers to control their money. It really is far more convenient for the banks.

This illustrates what an effective mass sales pitch can do to individuals within a captive herd. Worse yet, it is the unified herd of banks that share lobbying influences over the rule makers. This allows them to operate almost like a cooperative oligopoly.

Changing Times, Changing Beliefs, Changing Minds

Most of what we commonly share in our earthly pool of knowledge has evolved over a long period of time. I say evolved because, as you know, ours is a dynamic world and things do change. Sometimes change takes place over generations. Other changes can alter civilizations instantly.

History, science, language, and even math evolve along with the vast and ever expanding access to mankind's pool of knowledge. All of these changes affect the development of what is universally and personally perceived and believed. More than the facts themselves, it is the flood of ever-evolving interpretations of facts that modify entire belief systems.

Okay then, back to normal. Normal is really just a relative value judgment commonly accepted by the herd's members. Suppose you were raised in a shack, located in an area of nothing but shacks. Shacks would be normal to you, but only if you never ventured outside of that neighborhood. If exposed to the reality that most people aren't raised in shacks your perception of normal would obviously be altered. And, to those who are raised in a neighborhood of mansions, a neighborhood of shacks certainly isn't normal.

Until we are exposed to, and more importantly, comprehend other possibilities, our truth and our reality are limited by the parameters of our awareness and preexisting beliefs. Expanded awareness is one of the primary catalysts of change.

That Pesky Old Persuasive Credibility

Why do we embrace the thoughts, opinions and ideas of our oh-so-persuasive leaders? Are our leaders wiser or are they just more effective pitch artists? They could be both, but are they deserving of the credibility we bestow upon them simply because of their ability to persuade? If we perceive them to be credible, we become susceptible to their beliefs as well as their persuasions.

Credibility is one of the principal components of persuasion. The small segments of our society that exude the most credibility are the "winners." I say small segment of our society because winners comprise a very small portion of our population.

Let me first explain exactly what I mean by "winners" and why there are comparatively few. Winners are the ones who finished first. They beat everyone else at what they were competing for. Examples would be: the one who got the job or position, the one who came in first in a contest or game, the one who was chosen to represent others, the one who bested all in some form of competition, etc.

Those who did not get the job, didn't come in first, were not chosen and were beaten in a competition, by definition, lost. Because they lost in whatever event or individual circumstance, they, again by definition, became losers. How many football teams won the Super Bowl last year? Only one. The rest of the teams, once again, by definition, are all losers. How many people won the presidency? Only one. The rest of the candidates became losers.

In almost every scenario imaginable, the number of losers vastly outnumbers the number of winners. As a matter of fact, we are primarily a society of losers. This is the main reason that winners are perceived as stronger, smarter, faster, more knowledgeable, etc. This makes them more respectable and, as a result, more credible. With more credibility comes a perception of superiority. Perceived superiority yields an increased ability to persuade.

Bottom line: people believe winners and doubt losers. In doing so, we become susceptible to believing a winner's beliefs. We listen to, and actually believe, famous movie stars when they express their opinions about causes and political or religious ideologies. These are people who have successfully made their living pretending to be someone else. This surely tests the limits of our gullibility.

Both herds and individuals are attracted to winners. Herds follow winners. Herds believe winners. Members of a herd have been known to willingly subordinate their own values and beliefs to those of a winner. Since most people in a herd are not readily identified as winners, most herds are comprised of people who must therefore be identified primarily as "losers." By this I mean losers in the sense that they do not win enough to be considered credible. Remember, without some degree of credibility it is difficult to present an effective sales pitch.

By either some quirk of human nature or pressures inherent in almost all societies, people are attracted to winners and strive to be associated with them. This creates a self-imposed image that this somehow makes us winners by association. When the hometown or even the home-state sports team wins the national title, the pride felt by the fans makes them feel as if they are the winners too. The mere facade or pretense of success, credibility, and thus persuasiveness can be an extremely compelling sales pitch.

A credibility-based sales pitch requires the herd fall for the credibility in order for the follow-up sales pitch to be taken seriously. I mean, really, how can a sales pitch be successful if the source can't successfully sales pitch himself (or herself) as being credible? Good luck getting the herd to buy into that one.

When enough successful "winners" coalesce into a herd, the sales pitches generally become more of a directive. When one "winner" delivers a sales pitch, many buy in. With repeated sales pitch success comes a reinforcement of the "winner's" ego. If a group of these egos coalesces into a group, something odd takes place. An emergence of a giant, pseudo credible ego-monster begins to transform the sales pitches into ultimatums, dictates and doctrines. Ladies and gentlemen, I give you the incredibly credible "winners elite clubs," i.e., congress and its subcommittees, corporate boards of directors, world sports committees, school boards, the supreme court, etc. These groups of winners are the diminutive herds that herd the massive herds. The directive nature of their sales pitches has the power to shift the beliefs and actions of entire populations. They can even entice throngs of people. Look at the people who line up for holiday sales, rock concerts and iPhone releases.

As for the ultimate power of groups over individuals, always remember, our Supreme Court has ruled that corporations have some constitutional rights—just like people. So, in the old vintage 1973 movie Soylent Green, where people who die are secretly turned into the food source for the general population, Charlton Heston was wrong. "Soylent Green" isn't people. Corporations are people. (If money is speech, how much does free speech ultimately cost?)

Herds are also malleable and sometimes susceptible to ideological change. All it takes is the right circumstantial sales pitch. Both internal and external forces can manipulate or sway the beliefs of an entire herd. The exposure of a flaw in the premise of the sales pitch that originally bound the herd can dismantle the binding, cohesive fabric that held it together. Early in the 2015 Republican primary, Jeb Bush was the presumptive choice of the Republican herd. Donald Trump singlehandedly sales-pitched the herd into a completely different direction with boisterous criticisms and outrageous opinions that lacked any substance or policy direction.

This tactic was instrumental in successfully eliminating the rest of the field of contenders as well. In the opposing party's herd, Hillary Clinton's personal cellphone server faux pas left the democratic herd disjointed and scrambling for excuses and justifications. This kind of disillusionment often leaves a herd yearning for an alternative sales pitch they can passionately buy into.

So, do you choose to move with the herd or go it alone and think for yourself? Criticism in the form of a targeted sales pitch from a "perceived" credible source is infinitely more persuasive and alluring than a weak sales pitch from a truly credible and experienced source. Without experience there are no flaws to exploit, with experience there is. So inexperienced popularity will always win out over pragmatic rhetoric emanating from one with vulnerable experiential exposure. There is simply more opportunity to build one's self up by tearing the other down. The "uniformity and conformity of popularity" and the "popularity of uniformity and conformity" will both usually lead to the uniformity and conformity of all.

Security

No worries. That's right, "no worries" is the essence of security. Uncertainty, fear and worry are the anxious conditions that lack of security propagates. Security is really just an ongoing level of safety and monetary contentment that allows for a reasonably unimpaired access to needs, wants, socio-economic independence and unconstrained autonomy.

One of the prime ingredients in personal security is access to money. Money is also a prime instrument of force that affects the herd dynamic. It facilitates the acquisition of human needs, wants, desires and influence within the herd. Money is the medium of exchange that allows us to move beyond the realm of barter. It also serves to facilitate, or at least empower, enable, solicit and provide us with a fulfillment of our desire for the primal forces of nature. Without it you cannot successfully interact with, or even be an active member of, the herd. Money is one of the determinants of your value within most herds. In addition to security, money provides a proportionate degree of stability and control. Stability and control can, in turn, provide for the accumulation of additional money and thus additional security.

If you're human and reside somewhere in the civilized world you've been conditioned to need or want stuff. (Conditioned is another word for "habitual sales pitch acquiescence") To get stuff you're going to eventually need money. The question then becomes: What price are you willing to pay for this money?

Again, why do you want money? Well, it's not really the money you want. What you, and everyone else, really want is what the money can provide: security, food, shelter, transportation, power and, of course, a whole bunch of "things." Again, money is just a medium of exchange in our need/want fulfillment paradigm. The acquisition of things, transfer of ownership and the ability to obtain the necessities of life without employing direct trade is made possible by utilizing money. The amount of demand for "things," "stuff" and various intangibles is what establishes the value of money. Inflation doesn't make "things" more or less expensive. It makes money less expensive. Because inflation makes money less expensive, you can buy more of it with less stuff.

What do you think others are willing to pay you for your money? Just maybe they are willing to buy your money with a bunch of stuff they have. If their stuff isn't the stuff you want, maybe they can talk you into selling your money for stuff that they convince you to want. And isn't that what it's all about? There's nothing quite like the direct implementation of a sales pitch to acquire money.

In addition to the acquisition of stuff, money is a primary medium of exchange for influence, power, authority and control. It is also an influential ingredient in many forms of manipulation and persuasion. With the right amount of money a proportionate level of fear can also be instilled to enhance the effect of its controlling impact. This is one reason why money and power are often perceived as being interdependent.

Be Very Afraid

As powerful as money is, it is the element of fear that stands out as one of the supreme sales pitch manipulation devices. He who controls the money has the ability to both deprive and to enable through the employment of fear. Fear, when used to control, simply generates a more effective influence than deprivation alone. The ability to implant fear can certainly be acquired or purchased with money. The implanting of fear equates directly to the deprivation of safety, stability and security. That ability to deprive, once again, is a social, political and economic definition of power.

Other than that, money is just paper, metal pieces or a digital reference to a nebulous value held in cyberspace. Its scarcity remains a major annoyance, irritation and inconvenience to a majority of the population. It certainly is to me. Incidentally, money can buy happiness—but only if you can find the secret places where they're selling it. More than happiness, what money can buy is a degree of security.

A cumulative depletion of personal security within a society (herd) gradually leads to a weakened economic structure in the lower classes. If left to erode it can negatively affect the middle class as well. This isn't limited to economics. Stresses along social levels are also a result of decreases in security. A macro example of the effect on an individual would be when a downturn in the economy results in business layoffs. When enough employees in a community are terminated from their jobs the entire community suffers. As the employee's security is diminished, the community's security is diminished, and the security of the larger economic structure is diminished.

The loss of security exacerbates the former employee's range of options. Without the security of steady employment an individual becomes constrained or hindered in their ability to commit to a thirty-year mortgage, a five-year car loan or even a yearly apartment rental contract. Even if there were a desire to engage in the risk of debt, the availability of required credit would be diminished. On the social side, without a promise of at least some degree of security, even a marriage proposal loses some of its lure. Without security the number of out-of-wedlock births and single-parent families begin to increase.

On the herd level, a decrease in security eventually results in an increased degree of desperation. Without means to satisfy needs and wants, a sense of desperation infects the herd. One consequence of economically induced depression is often a learned helplessness exacerbated by a diminished access to security. Communal insecurity does in fact produce an escalation in crime rates, as well as other negative social behavior. Increased crime rates can ultimately result in residential and small business properties being vacated and community governmental coffers being depleted.

When the working class's security is removed, impoverished communities are commonly the result. Sure, there are those relatively few who persevere, but in situations like downward economic spirals, few emerge unscathed. I submit that the 2008 great recession stands as a testament to this hypothetical scenario. This type of situation is generally a consequence of sales pitches perpetuated over several years at the very top policy-making levels by very experienced and extremely well-financed pitch artists. I don't think much has changed since Charles Dickens eloquently opined about these very conditions.

The economy never fails to recover from this. It does so largely through a lowered cost of money and a more controlled approach to risk, which, in turn, produce slow but steady increases in productivity and demand. This return to stability is both a cause and an effect of an increase in security at the lower end of the economic spectrum.

Handouts seldom, if ever, remedy the long-term security of a herd or its members. The balanced, symbiotic relationship between production and demand has almost always provided the stabilizing effects of security. Most economists agree that somewhere between 70 and 80 percent of our economy is consumer driven. "Consumer driven" is the demand side of supply and demand. If a large enough portion of this consumer group is deprived of its security, the demand side of the equation becomes less stable. So I guess if everyone increases his or her demands, the economy will thrive. Okay, I meant demand, not demands.

Are You Happy Now?

Several studies have shown that people in some societies who live below what we consider to be the poverty level are far happier than successful people in our more prosperous competitive society. Why? Gee, I don't know. Could it be the lack of stress coupled with inherent security? Or could it be not wanting, having or doing what we've been told to want, have or do?

No study has ever shown that having everything you want ultimately makes you happier or more satisfied. In fact, every study shows the opposite. Simply "doing," more often than not, proves more fulfilling than "having." But we, in our infinite wisdom, or maybe because of a sales pitch, direct our efforts toward the pursuit of monetary gains to acquire possessions that we've been told will provide happiness.

We discover it's the effort we expend that provides most of our happiness. Happiness is often the result of purposeful life-fulfilling effort and fruitful accomplishment. Happiness doesn't necessarily produce money, and money doesn't necessarily produce happiness, yet this is what universal sales pitches for money and happiness promote. Pretty darned paradoxical and ironically profound, huh?

If money is the root of "all evil," then where does this "all evil" grow? I could certainly use some of its root. They must grow in that elusive forest of money trees.

Credit and Debt: The Ultimate Economic Control Over the Herds

Yes, credit and debt are a part of money's role in a human being's interaction with the herd. It didn't use to be that way, but, as primal forces of nature go, neither did ecology or visits to the dentist.

Credit is money you don't have right now but have convinced others you will someday have. Of course this credit is only available at a cost of additional money. Debt is that nasty bunch of monetary obligation that credit creates. Credit and debt are the ugly twin sisters that a need for additional money spawned. Credit and debt are also business's, as well as society's, primary source of money.

Money begins as debt when banks borrow it from the Federal Reserve. Investment banks were set up to invest this money. Commercial banks, on the other hand, primarily existed to make loans to businesses and individuals. Very simply put, personal and consumer credit allow for personal and consumer loans and thus personal debt.

Personal and consumer debt is a financial imprisonment we gladly accept in order to fulfill our craving for immediate comfort, social standing, status and "stuff," i.e., needs and wants. It replaces the rewards of our production with a promise of future production.

It's an enabling factor that allows our social herd to be dutiful consumers by facilitating acquisition of wants without the imposition of immediate payment.

With credit we can live where we want in homes we can't afford to pay for outright. We can own the car that suits our personality and not our wallet. And because of the little plastic cards we've all become dependent on, we can dine at exclusive restaurants and take fun-filled family vacations that wouldn't really be practical if we had to pay up front. We get to live beyond our means by gambling with our future. And all of this immediate need and want-fulfilling consumerism benefits the socio-economic structure of our entire cumulative herd.

Business credit and debt are a little bit different animals. They are the necessary financial grease that allows for the functioning and growth of the world's business, industry and banking enterprises. The true sales pitches here involve the rules that dictate the extent of control over the financial institutions and who exactly wields it. Think of it as the ultimate mega-mammoth Monopoly game.

A Couple of Paradoxical Cause/Effect Credit Conundrum Paradigms

If the economy crashes, as it did in 2008, the economic powers that be simply take everything away and we get to start all over—without all that credit. Oops.

I guess consumers and small businesses didn't see the ramifications of that tricky credit sales pitch, did they? The banks didn't either, but it worked out quite well for them because the national tax-paying herd was unwittingly forced into participating in a bailout that allowed the banks to maintain their solvency and good credit. As with most good sales pitches, there's the ubiquitous "but wait there's more." The more in this case: Your kids can all still go to college.

This brings us to a series of some of the best supply and demand credit sales pitches of all time. College loans are available to almost anyone who wants one. This requires a massive pool of money for college students to borrow from, and since the annual herds of graduates have few, if any, recourses to even begin making loan payments, they represent a large risk. Fear not, the financial sector lobbied, i.e., sales-pitched, our lawmakers into making student loans unforgivable. And, for the typically shortsighted student, this is truly unforgivable. In this case, what unforgivable means, is that students have no remedy, other than death, to mitigate their inability to pay back these loans. The debt remains in place until it is either completely paid off or, as just stated, death intervenes.

Unlike every other personal, business, corporate or even federal loan, there is no avenue or legal mechanism that can limit, readjust, forgive or undo the student loan debt, other than the lender's altruistic and compassionate benevolence. (Pause here for a quiet chuckle or, if you currently owe on a student loan, a furrowed brow born of genuine concern.) These loan parameters render the old adage: "The only certainties are death and taxes," obsolete.

Obviously, this type of loan got the lenders trampling all over each other to get in on this guaranteed, no risk, monetary plunder fest. Student loan funds suddenly became abundant. These easily accessible loan dollars resulted in an increase in demand for a seat at the college dining table. The money that fueled this increase in demand allowed colleges and universities to raise the tuitions to meet their own demand for these new loan dollars.

This, of course, created a greater demand for even larger loans. But it's okay; the colleges only raised the tuition by the amount of the newly available student debt. Since the volume of the available loans allowed the colleges to increase tuition higher than the inflation rate, it pretty much guarantees that most students will be stuck with their college debt for a long, long, long (sometimes life) time. Even taxes aren't as conditionally restrictive or restraining. What a sales pitch it must have been to get that one passed.

It would be a daunting task to change this cycle now. The job market demands more college degrees. Lenders bear little or no risk and it provides an ever-increasing pool of money to satisfy every university's thirst for even more of this money. Tuitions increase. More money is needed to attend. Loan amounts increase. With even more student debt the cycle repeats and perpetuates itself.

A good number of students actually do default. They default because they are either unable to find work in their field that pays enough to pay the loan and still allows them to live, or they aren't able to find work at all. If they default, their credit is diminished. Since most employers and landlords can now reject applicants based on poor credit scores, delinquent student loans can actually hinder the ability to find employment and housing. Now don't you fret now, when a student defaults on their loan, the government pretty much has the lender covered—not the student, mind you—just the lender.

Do you suppose the reason the total amount of student debt far exceeds the total amount of US credit card debt is because student debt is guaranteed? Who said there is no such thing as a "no risk" investment? It's not quite, but almost as risk free as the "bail out" protected banks. Now that's what I call a captive herd.

In the ultimate misuse of debt contest, there's a tie between paying off gambling losses and using debt to pay off other debt. If you get that financed at a lower interest rate you can make payments on both, but only if your interest in doing so is high enough.

SECTION THREE
The Pitch Masters
{Who, What, Why, How and When to Believe}

The Power to:
Herd the Herds / Manipulate the Masses
Guide the Groups / Motivate the Multitudes
Convince the Crowds / Sway the Swarms
Direct the Droves / Persuade the Populace
Control the Country
and Ultimately Rule the Realm

Chapter Eight
– The Want Fulfilling Marketplace –
Mankind's Monetarily Motivated
Manipulation Mechanisms

The Retail Distribution Of Preferences

Several years ago I owned a company that published and distributed a line of greeting cards. We had distribution in all but a couple of states and the entire line sold exceedingly well. The primary reason for the exceptional performance was an exhausting two-year test market that was undertaken prior to distributing the line nationally. The interesting thing about greeting cards is that each card must sell itself. It must stand on its own to entice a prospective customer to execute a purchase. The marketing allure must be inherent in each card.

Before I even started the company I had designed and authored six or seven dozen cards. The initial test market was more of a survey. This is where my (pseudo) brilliance was validated. People were shown each card and asked if it was something they would purchase. At that time they were labeled "Relationship Communication Cards".

Even though some were rather negative, they were all geared toward relationships. The verse on the front of one of the cards read: "The place I like you least ..." The inside caption read, "... is on my back." Interestingly, the majority of people surveyed replied with something like, "Oh yea, I would definitely buy that. I have someone who I'd love to give that to."

We went to press and printed out enough for a legitimate test market. This is where my brilliance, along with my ego, was smashed to bits. Only two cards in the line sold well. All of the others performed miserably. I had obviously misjudged the market and my ego paid the price. I had put out a product I believed everyone would want. Even the people surveyed believed they wanted them. My less than astute expectations of people's wants crashed head on into reality. I learned that people's actions are sometimes at odds with attitudes they may agree with.

Two years of drastic refinement was all it took for my attitudes and beliefs to totally realign with people's "real" wants, i.e., the wants they would back up with a purchase. The line was renamed "Special Thoughts" and by the end of the test market the entire revised line of cards sold exceptionally well. There was only one of the original "negative" cards that stayed in the line, but it too was replaced after a short period. That card read, "I don't like liver, spinach, cabbage ..." on the cover and "... or your attitude lately" inside. To this day I can't explain why people bought it. I learned to believe in what people will actually do over and above what they say they will do.

One of my more successful retailers opened my eyes to one of the primary reasons for this success. She revealed a philosophy that few, if any, of my thousands of retailers embraced. When purchasing inventory for her store she would buy one-third of what she really liked, one-third of what she didn't really care for and one-third of what didn't really affect her one way or the other. She informed me that each category sold equally well. By contrast, the retailers who only bought inventory they liked were markedly less successful.

This is what happened to me during my test market. I wrote and designed cards I thought people would buy. My personal opinions alienated a bunch more people than they attracted. This paradigm represents one of the golden rules of sales pitching, i.e., attempting to sell people what they don't want is immeasurably more difficult than selling them what they do want.

The test marketing also taught me that something as simple as the wrong word can severely limit the potential market of a product. When writing verse for my cards I became keenly aware of the limiting effect of inadvertently excluding market segments. Analysis of the test market proved this.

It was easy to overlook the exclusionary impact a few words can produce. The singular "I wish you the very best ..." would limit sales by excluding the entire market of the plural form of "we" or "us." This simple oversight actually produces un-selling instead of selling. As a result, the exclusionary "I," "we" and "us" cards were rewritten to become more inclusive to a larger segment of the market. The costly lesson I learned was that it's hardly ever a good idea to unnecessarily exclude potential customers from a sale pitch.

On the flip-side, I received feedback from people who gave praise for verse even when my aim was totally out of sync with the meaning they'd gleaned. Since they were customers, their intent was paramount. I still believe most people want to be included in the marketplace. Otherwise they have nothing to satisfy their desire to buy "stuff."

Marketing and Advertising: The Spells We've Grown Comfortable Being Under

How else are people going to know what they want if advertisers don't tell them? The true strength of successful advertising and marketing lies in the ability to appeal to vanity and ego with a promise of self-fulfillment, health, primal gratification and/or security. I mean really, who among us can resist the lure of somehow becoming personally enhanced?

Marketing and advertising are mighty forms of communication and belief-conditioning that we've all succumbed to. Feeling exploited? You should. After all, aspirin is aspirin, unless, of course, one brand has been presented convincingly enough to alter your belief.

Establishing credibility with a credible source presents a far more potent sales pitch than simply offering facts. Nobody really wants facts. Facts are boring. What people really want is the comfort of personal reassurance and status. These, we are told, are the true paths to happiness. And nothing provides reassurance and comfort better than the credibility of a dazzling sales pitch. If not the credibility then certainly the constant repetitive bombardment of those old feel good promises.

Advertising: The Seductive Mental Temptress

The entire advertising industry is based on the premise that enough individuals can be manipulated into doing something that it will result in a profit for their client. In other words, a certain percentage of people can effectively be told what to think, where to go, what to do and what to want. This will produce transactions involving monetary exchanges and a flow of revenue that not only increases the wealth their clients but also the wealth of the economy.

Advertisers are acutely aware that we are vulnerable to suggestions that we can have what they tell us we need or want. And, as the sheer volume of these life-directing forces numbs us, we won't even be aware of it. If we've learned anything, it's that advertisers, marketers, governments, religions and our relatives know a great deal more about what we want and need than we do. I mean really, we can't even go to a professional sporting event without being prompted by blaring speaker systems and motion-inducing light shows that tell us exactly when to cheer. And the entire crowd dutifully and repeatedly responds, right on cue, every time.

We're talking serious sales pitch response control here. The advertising emanating from the pharmaceutical industry is so powerful it compels people to pressure others to act on their behalf. I am referring, of course, to prescription drug ads. We can't personally respond to these advertisements. So we take our self-diagnosed ailment to the only one who can grant us permission to acquire these drugs. With any luck we have doctors intelligent enough to tell us to stop watching the ads and listen to them instead.

It's hard to figure where civilization would be without advertising. How would we know what we want? Where would television networks and producers get the money to entertain us? We would have to rely entirely on doctors to tell us which medications to take. Heaven forbid, what if we ever needed to find an attorney and how on earth could we ever make a decision on what beer to buy for our parties? How would websites subsist without the sponsorship provided by advertisers?

So we thank the advertising industry for informing us about everything they know we want, if only because they told us that we want it.

The $ and Sense of Convincing the Herd

The advertising and marketing industry is the obvious king of modern day mass commerce sales pitching. Advertising is more than a $180 billion per year industry in the US alone. It exists primarily to convince you that you too can become accepted by simply purchasing stuff. All you gotta do is buy into what they're selling.

My friend, $180 billion is an incredible amount of sales pitching. This means that over $600 for each and every man, woman and child is spent each year to convince them that they can obtain something that will improve their esteem or increase their level of comfort. The advertisers are willing to fork over this tidy sum because advertising and marketing works, and it works really well. Because it does work so well, advertising has crept into every nook and cranny of our lives. The advertisers are becoming increasingly effective at keeping their audio and visual messages perpetually in the path of our perception.

A great deal of the cost of advertising goes toward market research. Market research utilizes data collection involving how many of which category of people in which demographic will most effectively succumb to any number of various sales pitches. Along with buying habits, geographical and socio-economic territories or statistical analysis of targeted interests, marketing research gathers data mostly on you.

Marketing firms take great pride in knowing more about what you want than you do. The result is that you are often specifically targeted with sales pitches that facilitate the aforementioned deliberate and oftentimes subconscious, "All you have to do is," sales pitch theme. This simple and easy-to-accept sales pitch theme takes advantage of our susceptibility to the easy fix as well as our demand for acceptance and status regardless of the product or service. "All you gotta do" is just keep on wanting. And it doesn't really matter what it is you think you want, just keep wanting and they will eventually tell you exactly what it is you want.

There's nothing quite like a monetarily driven belief system, is there? How else could an entire economy sustain itself without convincing its members what they need to acquire in order to be liked, comfortable or live a happy life? This economic delusion presupposes that it's our financial duty to make ourselves acceptable or desirable in order to perpetuate our society?

I mean, if we don't spend, we could be weakening our nation. Is everything we buy into a result of traditional obligation, need satisfaction, peer pressure, status seeking or plain old patriotism? My vote has to go for traditional nationalistic obligation. Its more economically patriotic. Doesn't it make you feel like consuming is somehow contributing? No?

The Power of Suggestion

The power of suggestion is sometimes even more effective than a suggestion of power. Effective advertising actually implants the suggestion of a possibility into the brain. This suggestion requires the brain to evaluate and make a decision. This happens instantaneously and almost subconsciously. If the brain stimulus is effective, a motivation is created. This motivation is either acted upon or stored away for possible future action.

Advertising taps into what is relatively the same impulse that motivates people to either join into or follow the crowd, a group or even a belief. If the brain is not actively stimulated the suggestion is ignored and life goes on. The goal of the advertisers lies in what sales people call a numbers game.

An effective ad will reach many brains. If the percentage of brains that are stimulated is sufficient, the resulting monetary activity will justify the advertisement, i.e., the sales pitch will have worked and the money used to buy the ad will have been well spent.

There are two types of advertising. The first is "image," which explains or describes how or why a product or service is better than the competition. "Our hamburgers are the yummiest because we use the highest fat content." It's a presentation of advantageous characteristics and an enticing demonstration of general superiority.

The second type of advertising is a "call for action," which is the "act now or you'll miss out" pitch. "Call today," "for a limited time only," and "limited quantities on sale now," are a few typical examples. Or, in the case of the hamburger joint, "Better come in today. Our 'indigestion burger special' ends soon."

The entire advertising and marketing industry is comprised of companies directed by their clients to convince you to provide them with customers so they can make a profit. Over the years they've become adept at utilizing both of these time-tested and extremely effective presentation techniques.

Obviously, we've been conditioned throughout our entire lives to succumb to the bewitching call of advertising and marketing, whatever form it takes.

Sure, there are needed products and services that would never be known without the ads that make us aware of them. Nevertheless, all advertising is awareness-based sales pitching.

It is the competition for this awareness that perpetuates the marketing and advertising industries. But still, we consumers have all been conditioned to be at least subliminally attentive to the prospects presented in advertising. If this conditioning weren't extremely effective, there wouldn't be a multi-billion-dollar marketing and advertising industry.

Yes, we are all like trained monkeys and rubes that have been compelled, or at least influenced to acquire a great many things we could just as easily do without. They have effectively trained us to want even more than we already wanted to want. You don't believe me? Why then do the majority of national and state lottery winners completely deplete their winnings within only a few years? I guess it's like the rich guy's will stated after he died penniless. "Being of sound mind, I spent it all."

The majority of advertising exists to make you believe that by simply utilizing a product or service you will look and feel socially acceptable, or more suggestively, you will be somehow altered or transformed into a replica of the strong, beautiful, successful or famous people glorified in the advertisements. With apologies to the out of shape, perpetually exhausted, socially deprived single outsider: The use of a product or shopping at that particular store will not result in making you look like a super model, gain social acceptance or help you succeed.

Effective ads create illusions that lure people into associating with the positive effects of a product or service. These illusions can also create an expectation by the susceptible members of the audience that these effects can or will transfer to them. However, the probability of fully realizing the positive effects, so disingenuously illustrated in most ads, is dubious at best. But it is exactly this alluring possibility that is the effective part of the sales pitch.

As stated before, human beings are programed to pursue and maintain a certain level of comfort. Believing is comfortable. To maintain some self-control over these "comfort-based" beliefs, people routinely condition themselves to believe only what they want to believe. When the mind is closed to other beliefs it falls into the realm of bias, prejudice, predisposition and close-minded alienation.

When confronted with the possibility of comfort and the opportunity to believe that it's readily available, people not only buy in, they stay bought in. The advertiser's purpose is to tap into this desire for comfort by inferring, implying, promising or even "guaranteeing" you satisfaction and/or acceptance. This produces that impulse to procure. Both satisfaction and acceptance are some of the most desirable forms of comfort. The advertiser's job is to let you know that you are already wearing the ruby slippers. All you have to do is believe (the pitch, of course), click your heels together three times and voilà, all of the comfort you so desire will be yours.

"But wait, there's more." These advertising and marketing persuaders have some effective helpers. One of the most effective is social pressure. Social pressure is what we actually trained ourselves to succumb to back in our youth. You remember, status and that pesky need to belong. These were the youthful behaviors that sowed the seeds of real world social and economic competition.

We evolved but had already become eternally susceptible to the pervasive dynamics of "keeping up with the Joneses," or "wanting for the sake of having" or worse yet, still desperately wanting to impress the really cute one. All of these subtle motivations feed the research departments of each and every marketing and advertising entity.

Please pardon the reiteration, but once again the most sought after obsession in our "free market" society is "status." This is primarily because "absolute power" is beyond what most of us can realistically attain.

Seriously, can you imagine a sales pitch that said, "If everyone on earth had all of the gold that they wanted, everyone would be rich?" Logically, if you buy into the covet quest pitched by our culture, it wouldn't automatically reward you with a rich and happy life. If society removed all of the barriers to your every need or want, you would be no happier than would the citizens of a gold-laden population be wealthy.

Status, on the other hand, is that nebulous possession that seduces most of us into a desire to impress. So much so that we're willing to pay a bunch extra for "symbols" we believe will make us more impressive. As you may recall from the "Cool School Years" back in Chapter Three, the biggest, best and, more importantly, the coolest aspect in life is this subliminal refrain of status. It has been pitched to us as the essential ingredient required for ultimate happiness.

You remember, comfort and pleasure as opposed to pain and suffering. After all, if you're comfortable and have everything you want, and have eliminated everything you don't want, you must be happy. Even if people won't admit it, we envy those with status. And why not, they're the ones who get to play with all those really neat status symbols.

It should be noted here that status is merely an illusion that our brains have been sales-pitched into believing. One of the major ingredients common to both advertising and personal acceptance is this illusion of status. Put another way, status is the personification of complete and definitive expectation of recognition, acceptance and adulation attained through acquisition and ownership of envied possessions. Given the law of supply and demand, status is in the least supply and the greatest demand. That's what makes status symbols the most expensive possessions. And having lots and lots of money or power can certainly provide you with status. Even the illusion of having money or power can sometimes provide status. Almost everyone wants, or thinks they want, the accolades, adulation and respect that status provides.

The illusion and lure of status can be found in almost every type of advertised product or service. All of the most recognizable product names: Rolex, Ferrari, Gucci, Cartier, Trump, etc., are examples of status symbol brands. "The only way to prove you are the best is to possess the best" is one of the classic status seeker's supercilious mantras. We covet this status, not only because it's part of our evolved nature but also because it's our most efficient and effective gateway to being recognized as better or more important. Our cars, our dwellings and our vacation choices are all primarily based on status. We use it in our appearance: haircuts, makeup, jewelry and especially our clothing. We spend more on status than we do on food. Even some foods are for status.

We have been sold on the idea that each of us is measured or defined by how much, or what kind of, status we can afford to accumulate or display. Remember the comfort we all endeavor to maintain and the discomfort we struggle to avoid? The bombardment of a lifetime of sales pitches has rendered us a bunch of babbling seekers of comfort, trained to believe happiness and fulfillment can be attained through status.

This brings us to a relevant question: Are we freaking nuts? No, we're not really nuts. We are just exceedingly gullible.

It wasn't always like this. We evolved into this state of mindless acquisition gradually over a long period of time. The infant or child we once were still wants what it wants, when it wants it. It's just that now we've given into some pretty irrational reasons to want. Or didn't you see the advertisement?

A sibling of product-based status is "fame" status. Fame is simply mass acceptance and adulation through recognition of achievement. Actors, musicians, athletes, wealth builders, politicians and celebrities of all kinds are the players on the fame side of status seekers.

If you want to chase the "status through fame" dream, "all you gotta do is" work really hard at being the very best at something and/or have an incredible amount of talent or luck. But always remember the old saying I recently came up with, "All you gotta do is almost never all you gotta do." And because status is one of the most sought after level of acceptance, the victors of the world's social acceptance wars will have only the spoils of status to gain. All of this begs the question: If envy is purely a human trait, does it dehumanize us?

Establishing and Activating a Conditioned Response [Talk about captivating a herd...]

The following is a sales pitch hypothesis based primarily on my extensive market research. It's also a result of what I learned writing "topicals" in the promotion department of a local television station. "Topicals" are those enticing fifteen to thirty-second teases that highlight or advertise the stories that will be covered later on the news. So stay tuned. Oh, and by the way, whenever you encounter a principle, premise, assertion or conclusion in this book you disagree with, remember, "All you gotta to do" is disagree.

May I suggest that in order to justify your position you go ahead and study, analyze, hypothesize and validate, through research and testing, all of the sources of your facts and opinions to find a legitimate reason why your disagreement is more valid than my sales pitch. All while dismissing the entire accumulation of those unverified preconceived convictions that you have amassed. Or "all you gotta do is" allow yourself to buy into the following pitch.

When an elevated level of comfort or pleasure-based satisfaction follows a receptive response to a sales pitch stimulus, a desire to replicate this comfort is established. This state of contentment even creates a subconscious (or sometimes conscious) craving for ongoing patterns of repetition. In order to fulfill this desire to replicate the comfort, a comparable response to each corresponding sales pitch stimulus becomes increasingly automatic. Perpetually succumbing to an ongoing pattern is a conditioning to respond in order to fulfill the desire to replicate the comfort generated during the initial response. Like it or not, this is now a "conditioned response." The conditioning is complete when a response has evolved into a continuing pattern of repetition.

As one's behavior becomes conditioned to respond similarly to a sales pitch stimulus, a pattern of repetition is reinforced. Conditional sales pitches are those that are presented with conditions that attempt to assert power or control over you, i.e., kind of a conditional conditioning. These sales pitch conditions can result in subservient behavior and interfere with or even transform personal value systems and prejudices.

Herds generally advocate inherent conditions that often cause personal values to transform or evolve into institutional-based belief codependency. In other words, individual identity is sacrificed for the benefit of the group and the group identity, i.e., there will be consequences if you attempt to fight city hall (or any of the powers that control the herd).

The Mimic Effect

Have you ever felt compelled to participate in a standing ovation simply because several members of the audience stood up and clapped? Spontaneous impulses to imitate behavior are often a product of insecurity. It is so much easier to copy the actions of the herd than to face the potential discomfort of demonstrating contrasting or conflicting behavior. This discomfort is just a simple form of embarrassment, which is just another subtle form of fear. It's difficult to resist mimicking the actions of a group, even when it's a group of total strangers.

As individuals we follow the subliminal "instructions" of the herd because we've been inherently conditioned throughout history to do so. Those who want to lead or control the behavior of the herd know this.

Way back when Colonel Parker was managing Elvis, he understood the effect of behavioral imitation. During concerts early in Elvis's career, he would position several screaming and cheering young women close to the front of the stage. He did this to create excitement within the entire audience.

I'm sure Elvis would have been just as big a star without this ploy, but this little scheme has been duplicated by many in the entertainment industry with great success. It is an example of group manipulation by utilizing a "mimic effect" sales pitch. There are many variations of this type of mass manipulation marketing outside of the entertainment industry.

The same herding of behavior can be found in politics, religious faiths, social organizations and many other belief-based groups or populations. Regardless of the type of organization, it is all still just marketing to influence or control both group and individual behavior within the group.

I'll Tell You What

If a tree falls in the forest and no one is there to hear it, is there sound? Well, it depends on a mutually accepted definition of sound. If sound is defined merely as the existence of sound waves, then the answer is yes. If it's rightfully defined as the transmission and "reception" of sound waves then the answer is no. No reception; no sound. Similarly, a quick examination of the meaning of "communication" will yield a requisite inclusion of "reception."

In an upper level communication class back in college, we did a little experiment. Two desks were placed back to back. An identical bunch of tinker-toys were placed on each. A student was seated at each of these desks. The professor assembled the tinker-toys on one of the desks. The student whose back was to the professor was unable to see the assemblage. The student with the assembled tinker-toys was told to instruct the other student on how to identically assemble the pieces. The other student was not allowed to communicate at all.

In addition to being hilarious, the results, in every subsequent attempt were equally disastrous. Nothing even came close to matching the original.

In the second phase of this experiment, a limited number of specific questions and singular answers were allowed, but no open dialogue. This resulted in substantially greater accuracy, but still not an exact duplication. That wasn't achieved until an open and unlimited dialogue was allowed. Communication does not truly exist until the recipient fully comprehends the senders intended message. Confirmation of communication can only be verified through open dialogue.

Are our modern personal and mass communication methods evasive or invasive? It wasn't too terribly long ago, historically speaking, when people could only get what they couldn't produce for themselves through actual face-to-face human contact. We've certainly come a long way since then. Now you can order it, have it delivered and pay for it virtually with no human contact whatsoever. It seems that all of humanity is quite willing to accept this social exclusion paradigm, as long as our technologically advanced media devices agree to provide some degree of comfort through artificial companionship.

Communication Evolution

Never has isolation been so inclusive. Technology is so easy and it's capable of providing everything a human could want. Go ahead, you know you want it. Everything in the world you desire is packed neatly into the cell phone that's right there in your hand. Congratulations, the convenience that mankind has been striving for, ever since the Jetsons were introduced, is finally yours. This universal access device almost makes the decisions for you, doesn't it?

This access, by itself, is a pretty good sales pitch. It's a sales pitch you want because access to artificial human contact through social media is better than no human contact at all. Digital contact has actually become more comfortable than real human contact. If you don't believe me, just download any new Wi-Fi smartphone-compatible streaming reality series. And don't miss the latest episode of The Digitally Distracted Universe.

This is all brought to you by "I-thing-so" and "Samsung-tunes." In the next episode: The entire human race is threatened when direct human-to-human contact is rationed by digital rule. Will this lead to an inevitable decrease in human procreation? Is this the ultimate worldwide technologically induced omen? Stay digitally tuned for the next, and possibly last, episode. Hopefully this doesn't come to pass. Who would we leave our dysfunctional and sexually deprived planet to? Maybe someday technology will learn to procreate for us.

The News

"I'm mad as hell, and I'm not going to take it anymore"

Yes, the news has evolved into a form of entertainment and steadily forged its way into the realm of marketing and advertising. Network is a famous vintage movie of historical broadcasting significance. It foretold the transformation of news programming into a monetarily and politically influenced entertainment format. I say foretold because what the movie portrayed is exactly what has come to pass.

The movie illustrated the battle between pure journalistic integrity and the powerful influence of money-generating, entertainment-infused news programing. It exemplifies how money can, and often does, trump purpose. News is news, until you can commercialize it, opinionate it, politicize it, prejudice it, entertainmentize it and use it to further an agenda. News programming, when laden with superfluous adjectives, is generally nothing more than biased entertainment. On the other hand, uncompromising and thoroughly researched journalistic reporting, free of adjectives is, well, NEWS. So nowadays our "news" is mostly either entertainment or biased misinformation. The old saying, "No news is good news" is obsolete and without merit. "No news is actually bad news." Unless it's "fake news," in which case it's just the illusion of news.

As it stands now, all information-based mass communication is dependent on both the size of the soapbox and which way it leans. "My soapbox is cleaner and bigger than your soapbox, so obviously, I am the one who is right. Advertisements that tout the facts generally do the same thing investigative reporters do. The facts they do present are generally 100 percent correct. It's just that they never seem to present all 100 percent of the facts.

Being Liminal of the Subliminal

If your attentions have ever been lost in some mind-numbing made-for-television drama or series, drearily focused on the characters or the plot, there are forces etching their subtle message into our brain. These forces are known as product placements. During the comfortable, escape time, spent lounging on the sofa, have you ever become aware of some overtly displayed logo or brand name on the hero's car, laptop or beer can? These product placements are subtle sales pitches that product advertisers pay dearly for in order to create visibility. It's kind of a hyper-, mass-marketing word of mouth.

Word of mouth is one of the most effective forms of sales pitching. Hearing from a friend that a certain brand of toilet paper is more tush friendly is infinitely more effective than a pastel-colored cartoon bear pitching softness in a TV ad. When you see familiar characters in a weekly series or a major star in a movie, the bond is akin to friendship, albeit somewhat one-sided. The effect of a trust relationship lends credibility to their product brand preferences.

You're standing in the isle at the store and you're confronted with five different brands of the same product. The leading character in last week's episode of your favorite show used one of the five products. There's an extremely high probability that you'll choose that brand. You'll most likely do this, even though your perception of the product placement in the show was subliminal.

Sponsorship is a "word of mouth" form of product placement. (These products are used in race cars so they must be great.) You can hardly tell what color a Nascar driver's suit is because of the massive number of sponsor patches. Ski racers kick off one of their billboard skis and hold it up almost before they finish the race. There are so many Nike swooshes on pro team uniforms that a novice spectator might infer they all play for team Nike, which, in most respects, they do.

All of this has to do with how we relate to, idolize, associate ourselves with or fantasize about people who are great at the things we wish we could do. The only way to emulate their achievements is to buy the products they're paid to advertise. I still don't understand, after buying all of the things I have, why I'm not making millions dunking a basketball, throwing a touchdown pass, and winning a green jacket at the Masters. I mean hey, I drink what they drink, wear the same brand of underwear and, most importantly, the shoes. It's all in the shoes, you know. It better be, because after buying the shoes I certainly can't afford the same brand of car most of them are paid to drive. Hero worship does have its financial limits.

Another example of subliminal marketing is women's clothing. Over the years women have been subtly made to feel better by certain brands within the garment industry. By implementing an almost imperceptible upward alteration in sizing, women were made to believe they were getting smaller. With no change in actual size, women could miraculously fit into the next smaller size. Talk about providing personal comfort, this is something they could brag about. "I used to barely squeeze into a twelve. Now I am a perfect ten." You can see how this would work out for the companies without making the women work out.

Conformity Is for Wusses

Why do you suppose, that throughout the vast world of literary, theatrical and motion picture archives, both the heroes and the villains are almost always non-conformists, rebels or misfits? The characters displaying the greatest personal strength are those who shun the herd identity. Conversely, most people are content with safely embedding themselves in the comforting bosom of the herd. Oh the sardonic irony. Why is it we choose to ramble through this life content with our conformity? We all maintain a secret desire to be the hero of our own life at some point.

As conformists, most of us self-relegate ourselves to merely being the victims of our lives rather than the heroes. Most are content to vicariously "Walter Mitty" through life. The reinforcement of this conformity is what perpetually keeps our grand desires locked up inside ourselves. It starts out slowly, building on the conditioning of peer acceptance that we gleefully embraced throughout our school years.

This pressure and willingness to conform progresses naturally into the workplace and lodges itself firmly into our compliant little existence. Man, talk about the power of self-pitching. The revolutionaries among us rebel only to be recognized as non-conformists and are labeled as such. Either way, it's a facade to convince others to accept us based on who we futilely attempt to project ourselves to be. It's our profound and wishful self-pitch.

There are many times when conformity leads to risk aversion. Risk aversion is a self-imposed sales pitch that the outcome of either an involvement or an attempt will result in a greater loss than the potential gain. To many, risk is counterproductive to the preservation of comfort. In the afore-stated Nazi death camps, groups of prisoners concurrently conformed to the actions of the group when ordered to trudge toward what they knew was certain death. Paradoxically, the risks associated with defiance gave way to conformity in spite of the probability of identical outcomes.

When forced to choose between "conform and die" or "fight and die" in a futile situation, most surrender to a conditioned response of acquiescing to group comfort. The group is, subconsciously, a considerably more comfortable choice than fighting. The nonconformists are generally envied because they are almost always perceived as a person of strength.

Those who refuse to buy into the communal sales pitches are the individuals we often find to be either humanity's honorable heroes or its malicious villains. So few of us seem to possess the individual strength of character required to stand up to the authority of the herd. And so, in the interest of maintaining the comfort of our mundane existence, most of us simply acquiesce to the status quo of our security-driven conformity.

The Art of the Pitch

Most of the sales pitches in larger business transactions that I've been involved with were presented to me allegorically, or metaphorically. This is one method that elevates the presenter into a position of superiority. It creates a subconscious presupposition that a direct or overt sales pitch would obviously be too complex for the subject to understand, so the presenter creates an adult to child relationship through a storytelling simplification. The subtle subliminal assumption is that the subject needs a more easily understood or sympathetic presentation of the pitch. The inference, interpretation of a metaphor can be much more easily bought into than the subject of a direct pitch.

A story was offered during a presentation by a group of investors wishing to negotiate for a casino property my partner and I owned. The story involved a simple shoemaker, who was awarded the privilege of making boots for the entire army. In the story the cobbler was so overwhelmed with the complexities of producing on such a volume that he went broke and lost everything. This story was intended to demonstrate the immense complexities involved in building and operating a casino.

The insinuation of their metaphorical sales pitch was that we would be overwhelmed and thus go broke, if we didn't let them help us out by taking this property off our hands for cheap. We had three other similar offers. I say similar, not because they all involved the same story, but because they involved similar metaphorical lures that were meant to convince us that the inherent complications that developing a casino property presented made it worth far less than it really was.

Other subtle methods of inducement can involve forceful utilization of logic fallacies, unjustifiable justifications, or something as simple as rolling of the eyes or a facetious chuckle to poo-poo objections and, of course, flat out lies. Who amongst us hasn't, at one time or another, bought into a pitch that was based on a total fabrication? If you answered, "I haven't" then I applaud your ability to completely isolate yourself from political campaigns, talk radio, courtroom proceedings and teenage offspring.

Propaganda: The Epitome Of Unidirectional Herd Manipulation by Mass-Communication

The sales pitch that herds the herds. Propaganda is a uniting communication force that members of the herd can identify with and rally around. It's a communicated source of unifying comfort and directionally focused intent. The message usually serves as a rallying cry to those seeking the security and comfort of the herd.

For propaganda to secceed, it must be presented with content that's inherently indisputable. Propaganda takes many forms: overt bombardment of a directed message; news media's selective omission of opposing viewpoints or accounts of events; mass distribution of entertainment or music containing both subliminal and explicit expressions of biased opinions; even textbooks or curriculum that provide only narrow interpretations or biased agendas. Whether a democracy, a republic, a dictatorship, monarchy or a fascist regime, he who controls the information controls the populace. People who lack the ability or will to generate their own defensible opinions or positions will inevitably latch onto or be forced into the belief patterns that are provided for them by the leadership.

The mass sales pitching ability that propaganda provides has been exacerbated by unprecedented expansion in digital communication technology. The world's population is connected. Biased and opinion-based information proliferates in this deluge of global communication.

People naturally gravitate toward the like-minded sources. From small local book clubs to massive terrorist organizations, the introduction to and reinforcement of beliefs strengthens and reinforces these belief-based bonds. When the flow or content of information is controlled or compromised, the bias of a source is set free to influence a susceptible portion of the masses.

In countries or societies where access to this communication is stifled, suppression proliferates. Tension and distrust permeate and embolden the ranks of the rebellious, while bias and dogma-driven compliance inspire the masses of submissive followers.

Chapter Nine
— God vs. Religion —

Is God the same thing as religion? Would God approve of modern day religions? The answer depends either on your faith in your beliefs or your belief in your faith.

What to Believe and What to Believe In

What do you believe? Now why on earth would you believe that? Is "what you believe in" the same as "what you really believe?" How much of what you believe, or "believe in," have you verified as truly believable? By this I mean, what have you verified outside of your blind faith and the vast realm of blind faith that other people's opinions are based on? Are your beliefs based on reality or is your reality based on your beliefs? Honest and well-considered reflection of these questions will quite possibly result in answers that could make you just a little uncomfortable believing.

God, Deity, the Divine Supreme Being

If you don't already have one, this is where you get to choose a God. If you're like most people, your God has already been chosen for you. If that's the case, you were almost certainly imprinted mentally sometime during your "impressionable youth." If not, you may have been presented with choices that were possibly a little beyond a maturity level required to intellectually evaluate your options. But now you're old enough and wise enough to either choose another God or possibly a different religion that prays to the same God you already have. You can certainly stick with the God you have. Perhaps you would choose to choose no God at all. Even if you choose no God, it's ultimately your choice. But if you choose to believe there's no God, wasn't it God who bestowed upon you the arcane free will that allows you the capacity to make that choice? This is just one example of the many God conundrums that permeate the extensive list of "non-believer" justifications.

Most people are either totally content with the God they have or are too embedded in their deep-seated belief system that it renders them incapable of switching to another. Others seek a different God that may better fulfill or provide for their own philosophical, intellectual or ethereal needs. Isn't it puzzling how this placating and perplexing preponderance of paradoxical god stuff precipitates and perpetuates such permanency in personal perspicuous pomposity?

189

Who is this God fellow anyway? Where and when did you first learn of his (or her) existence? Who first told you about God? Is your source's knowledge of God first hand? Is your God a "someone," a "something," an "entity," a "phenomenon," a "philosophy" or merely a "concept?" Since human beings generally believe in one God or another, is your God one of the more popular gods? If you don't believe in any of the world's current list of gods: Christian, Buddhist, Jewish, Muslim, Hindu, tribal, etc., what God do you believe in? I'm going to guess the belief you have in God was initially planted in your brain somewhere back in the early years of your life. If not, someone or something has since influenced you to change. You don't actually believe you came up with this belief on your own do you? No way. Well, theoretically, if someone lived their entire life in a vacuum, it's certainly conceivable they could, through some nebulous thought process, mentally create a supreme being to believe in. Outside of that hypothetical, the reality is most of us were not only told by someone exactly who we should believe in, but also how and why. If these choices were presented or acted upon later in life, they were, more than likely, heavily influenced by a promise of comfort, security, contentment or forgiveness.

But Is It God's Religion?

Even the members of many non-religious families

acknowledge that some form of God may exist. Most people are brought up with a subtle understanding that both God and religion are essentially the same thing. Kind of like blending God, the word of God and the procedures of worshiping God into "Religion = God." The reality is, they really aren't the same thing. While God is God, religion is the practice of worship, praise and adoration combined with a ceremonial ritual or display of devout faith that is directed to God.

While God is God in most faiths, each religion's God may be just a little different than the others, if only in name. Most religions provide us with the instruction manuals on why, what and how we should believe in or worship that particular religion's God.

Religion also provides specific directives on which greater power the believers are to believe in. Almost all religions philosophically present human objectives as positive endeavors, i.e., be a good person, do good things, be kind to others and lead a moral and ethical life. I say almost all religions because, even in the twenty-first century, there still remain some who align themselves with religions that profess violence or death to all who do not believe in their God. This, in keeping with the historical aggressiveness of most medieval religious practices, is still a major source of suffering, conflict and war to this day. I mean, "My God is better than your God, therefore I must kill you" isn't very conducive to "Peace on earth and goodwill toward man."

With a leap of faith we may someday definitively find the answer to the eternal question: Did God really create man or did man create God? As it stands now, God only knows. I don't believe there is empirical or definitive evidence that would support or contradict either side of this conundrum. What we do know is that mere mortals created religion.

One reason we humans did this was because of frustrations brought about by not having a source to answer the unanswerable questions. Just as frustrating were the enigmatic questions that resulted in inscrutable answers that were either beyond human comprehension, human explanation or human control. This is the old "self-pitch cushion." It's really comfortable for humans to have God, the stars, luck, destiny, superstitions or any number of things to either conveniently give thanks to or to lay the blame on. Religion conveniently and effectively provides comfort through the structure of a pragmatically illuminating organization.

Another reason humans created religion was fear. Since the beginning of our species, humans have recognized that there is danger out there. Fear of this danger not only resulted in herding behavior but in the belief behavior of the herd. Herds deal with a fear of the unknown or unexplainable by believing in a greater power. Some of the earliest civilizations believed their gods resided in things beyond their scope of understanding.

The sun, moon and stars, the earthly elements like water, fire, wind, volcanoes, and great imagined animals were just a few of the gods that controlled or watched over their lives. Some ancient societies even worshiped the political and military leaders that ruled their lives as gods, as per the leaders' commands, of course. These early cultures were convinced gods—manifested in tangible creatures or objects—were responsible for all of the good and bad things that happen. They also believed that the gods were their source of protection, security and comfort. This was, of course, so long as they did not anger the gods.

In our somewhat advanced civilization it is easy to scoff at the idea that these multitudes or herds could be convinced that such mundane subjects were worthy of worship. In our modern world it would be folly to base our beliefs on tangible creatures or objects, except in the case of rock stars and movie stars. By believing them responsible for all of the good and bad things that happen, while also believing they were empowered to provide us with protection, security and, of course, comfort, we would be denying mankind's advancements in knowledge.

Our progression in scientific knowledge is primarily responsible for dismissing early gods. One can only hope that "scientific knowledge" isn't just another sales pitch. Over time, scientific study has revealed most ancient gods to be nothing more than what they are, i.e., imagination, matter or some existential idealistic symbols. And neither matter nor symbols are very capable of maintaining any supernatural, mystical or spiritual power over us. With respect to religion, it would seem that "matter" doesn't really matter.

Power is one of the common characteristics of most religions. Religions have been competing with governments for control over the populace, since both were first organized. History has some pretty compelling evidence to justify this conclusion. Most religions still maintain varying degrees of power over their eager and willing followers.

This power sometimes reveals itself overtly and dictatorially. In these types of religions the devotees are required to place the wishes, dictates and commands of the leaders above their own. The followers are reduced to the roll of servants to the will of their religious leaders and their interpreted religious doctrine. These are often referred to as radical or extremist religions.

An extremist religion's power is born of profound and narrow intolerances that are generally directed by the perpetuation of a cause-based ideology. Conversely, most of a peaceful religion's power is derived from providing meaning, security, hope and a promise that believing will provide comfort; that, along with a healthy dose of fear that only the threat of going to hell can generate. It provides yet another proof that mass sales pitching really does work.

Most religions of today are really more a presentation of interpretations of their original teachings than an accurate reflection of historical doctrine. As interpretations, and in most cases, reinterpretations, most religions have evolved into perpetual streams of ever-evolving modern day sales pitches.

The teachings have been adapted to modernized or updated sales pitches. But there are still sales pitches with ramifications that convey the same old "fire and brimstone" doctrine. If you don't believe in the teachings of this or that religion, you will still die, go to hell, lose your soul, or even possibly be stoned to death, etc. Alternatively, there are a few more contemporary religions that advocate getting stoned with others, rather than being stoned by others. Higher calling?

Some of the largest religions on earth have a history of torturing and killing the heretics who rejected teachings or refused to believe. A few religions still follow this practice today. Talk about a sales pitch of biblical proportion.

Flocking to the Shepherd

Peer pressure, guilt, promise of immortality or afterlife, material or spiritual security, and so on, are all part of the "carrot and stick" pitch of almost every faith. Those who believe hard enough can pitch others. The results of perpetual mutual group pitches are religions that comprise a majority of the human population.

Remember the group acceptance we struggled to attain back in school? We don't even have to try here. It's religion, we're all accepted. You should be getting that warm fuzzy feeling about now. With absolutely no effort at all, you can belong. But remember, anyone who doesn't accept this holy universal acceptance may be a sinner, a heretic or an outcast. But what's not to like? Most of the world's religions offer some form of incentive: immortality, heaven, nirvana, enlightenment, a bunch of virgins; sharing and forgiveness of sins; spiritual fulfillment and security; and most of all, purpose, i.e., a reason to lead a good and fruitful life. .

So come on down. You can sign up at your local church, chapel, synagogue, mosque, temple, cathedral or your choice of countless alternative places of worship. Unfortunately, the members of some religions get reincarnated as animals or even other people, hopefully not a barnyard animal or the offspring of those whackos who live down the street.

Blessings for Bucks

The total annual revenue of the world's religions and various religious organizations is approximately, well, a great deal more than a whole, or holy, bunch. Even governments aren't really sure how much money religions control. My limited research indicates that it's quite possibly a more massive sum than most of us can even imagine. I did some interesting research on a couple of religions and came up with a nebulous but still incredibly massive sum. While this only included a couple of religions, trust me when I say the construction of opulent temples, churches, mosques and synagogues hasn't significantly lightened the purse of any religion. We're talking massive amounts of God dollars here.

Where do these incredible amounts of money come from? Obviously they come from the masses, multitudes and herds of believers, followers and devotees. Is it from those who finance their faithfulness through the beliefs of their religion's teachings? Does it pour in from those who would purchase their peace of mind, pay off their guilt or even monetarily sacrifice for sins committed? Well, sort of.

Most of religion's financing comes from devout believers who donate, because it simply makes them feel better. Feeling better makes them comfortable and just a little more secure. And feeling better makes them happy. So giving money to a religion makes people happy. And you thought money couldn't buy happiness.

The Word of God

Is "the word of God" a sales pitch? Who actually wrote the scriptures, God or God's followers? As illustrated before, man created religion, so we could all have an organized process to follow in order to facilitate the worship of God. So, God creates man, man creates religion and religion perpetuates a following.

As a matter of fact, man created a lot of religions. And regrettably, it wasn't actually God, but rather apostles, disciples, worshipers and followers who provided us with their interpretations of "the word of God." For example, within the Christian Bible there are the teachings of men who told "in their own words" what they believed the word of God to be.

This is where "the word of God, according to" references specific authors of specific passages, chapters and verses. When packaged together with the passages, chapters and verses of other authors you end up with the Bible. The source? Interpretations and comparisons of the ancient Masoretic text and the Septuagint applied to the Dead Sea Scrolls.

Over the years, all of these passages, chapters and verses have been transcribed, interpreted, translated, re-interpreted and compliantly updated to the vast number of diverse publications of today's Bibles. Back when it was originally written, I'm pretty sure God's "Bible writers" didn't transcribe, word for word, in any of the modern European, Asian, English or tribal languages. So someone other than God had to, one assumes with the best of intentions, interpret the words and translate them without altering content, meaning or intent. Now how close to the actual word of God do you realistically believe the modern day Bible is? Since the original writings no longer exist, there's no way to know. In the end, "the word of God" is taken in good faith. And if your faith is really good and your faith is really strong, your God will obviously be the best really good and really strong God.

The Evangelical Pitch

The God debate is almost as old as the human race. If you believe, you believe. If you don't, you don't. However, to view things from a sales pitch perspective we can certainly reflect on many of these spiritual questions that we all sometimes ponder. Is there a need in each and every one of us that must be filled, or is it simply comforting to have a belief system that helps us to confront the harsh realities of living with all the bozos around us?

My intent here is certainly not to offend the believers of any religion, but, in the context of sales pitching, consider the following scenario. A non-believer receives a call from one of God's disciples.

The conversation could go something like this:

> "Hello. May I speak to the potential believer in the house?"
>
> "No, there are no believers here."
>
> "You're not a believer?"
>
> "No."
>
> "Man, are you missing out."
>
> "Yea right. Missing out on what?"
>
> "For one, all the comfort and security believing in a belief can provide."
>
> "What do you mean, believing in a belief?"

> "I mean God. God is the belief, and by believing this belief, you attain eternal salvation. In addition, all of the others who share this belief in God, can help you bear the heavy burden of your personal responsibilities. And the best part is, you will live forever in paradise. All you have to do is follow the teachings, and you belong. So, how about it? Wouldn't you love to share in all of the warmth and security a supreme being can bring to your life and then live forever in paradise?"
>
> "And all I have to do is agree to start believing in this belief?"
>
> "That's it. You get all of this with absolutely no cost to you... And there's more. If you sign up right now, we'll throw in a huge book that contains all of the beliefs written in God's own words."

Lacking any reasonable objections or compelling arguments to justify rejecting this offer, most people would sign right up. So yes, for better or worse, religion is, and always has been, a sales pitch.

Unfortunately, there are also the not-so-positive enticing motivators employed by religions. Both guilt and fear have been utilized extensively by all religions throughout history. Guilt and fear are also considered to be two of the ultimate methods of control used by governments and many other groups and organizations. These tools of control are generally employed when the disposition to control is a bit more tyrannical. The utilization of guilt and fear by almost all religions has been well documented throughout the history of mankind.

Life: It's to Die For

Is there life after death? Heaven? Hell? Don't know, never been to either of them. I haven't been to a lot of different countries either, but I have a pretty good idea they exist. There are scrolls, parchments, paintings, sculptures and, obviously, some big books that inform us of various forms of afterlife. Now, if God has a sense of humor, this afterlife stuff could all just be part of his standup routine. If not, this really could be serious stuff.

Now, not to be crass, but, as stated before, the Bible is either the word of God or just some book written by a bunch of guys who wanted people to believe that what they wrote was the word of God. Did God write a book or is this the ultimate sales pitch? If you don't buy into it you go to hell when you die. Oh, and by the way, if you try to disprove it or attempt to repudiate the sales pitch, you are labeled a non-believer, a heretic, or a social outcast, and you'll go to hell when you die. And, in a few religions, you'd be killed in order to facilitate a more rapid decent into hell. Ouch.

Are most gods heralded in the religions of the world benevolent, caring, wise, fair and just gods? Or are there gods who are more like demons? Is worshiping the Devil, satin, Beelzebub or whatever anti-God of choice, simply believing negatively or is it elevating the evil forces to the level of God? Well, my guess is that it depends on the sales pitch that gets bought into.

In Credible Beliefs

Is your entire moral foundation based on religion? Is your character defined by what divinity you believe in? Just keep the faith and you'll never lose faith. Search your mind. Search your heart. And, if you believe that you have one, search your soul?

Your mind is what you think with. Your heart (no, silly, not the organ in your chest) is what you feel with. Your soul, on the other hand, is something that I can pretty much guarantee you've been told about, i.e., sales-pitched.

Once you arrive at what you really believe, how confident are you in defending this belief? How close do you think your true and core beliefs are to reality. I contend that you believe they are just as close as you and others have convinced you they are. You further convince yourself by the positive reinforcement of not only many others but also the warm and comforting feeling derived from believing. Would you feel guilt or embarrassment if you scrutinized the realization that your entire belief system is based on things people told you when you were just a child? Do you cling to the spiritual teachings of others because it's more convenient to cling to the comfort that dependency and responsibility-sharing and sin-forgiveness afford you?

Guilt and personal responsibility certainly are heavy burdens. Do you believe only because it makes it easier to share these burdens? Is there religion? Absolutely. Is there God? God only knows. Yet there are those who believe in God but not in religion. Go figure. The result of belief without basis in fact is faith. Most people's viewpoints, values, opinions and beliefs are steeped in faith rather than facts.

Face it: faith is inherently more capable of providing existential comfort than facts ever could. "There are no atheists in foxholes" is a saying that's based in a human incapacity to individually deal with fear. Speaking with God can add a bit of comfort while taking the edge off the anxiety of facing eminent doom all alone. Religions will always flourish with or without God, because people will always need to believe in, follow and belong to groups that offer the promise of hope and make them feel safe, secure and comfortable. On the other hand, God only knows why some folks don't need or believe in God or religion.

Chapter Ten
– Politics and the Law –
The Enigmatic Application
of Questionable Morality

Since morals and ethics don't exist anywhere else in nature, do morals and ethics conflict with human nature?

Politics—The Sales Pitch And Negotiation Smörgåsbord

Welcome to the quintessence of master level sales pitching, negotiating and, of course, the manipulation of a totally biased, misinformed and gullible public. There are many separate facets of sales pitch skills that are required to succeed in the field of politics. First and foremost, there are a variety of compulsory sales pitches that are required to simply get into the game. Playing the political game is a step-by-step sales pitch process, where each step must be successfully completed before the next step can be taken.

Step one: Convincing the electors. The voters must be carefully and skillfully coerced into falling for a plethora of platitudes that will satisfy their idealistic expectations. I say idealistic because most expectations consist of ambiguous generalities that somehow disappear in the face of pragmatic realities, or when actually put to the test. A typical example would be in a presidential campaign.

Presidential candidates often espouse agendas that are outside of the purview of presidential powers. The president can't unilaterally implement a spending program. Congress holds the purse strings. So why do they say things like this? First off, it's a sales pitch to get elected and not a genuine promise. Secondly, it works because people desperately want to believe their leaders. If the sales pitch strategies are successful, the candidate wins, and the transition into step two begins.

Step two: Soon after successfully emerging from this first phase of pitching, a true politician must gain the respect of political peers in order to cultivate and secure those beneficially influential alliances. Convincing these cohorts to align, all while they are simultaneously posturing to gain favor with their own coalitions, is tantamount to an assemblage of pickpockets who all pick each other's pockets. This step must be perpetually undertaken while simultaneously re-implementing step one in order to maintain empathy with the electorate.

Step three: Attention now turns to sales pitching cohorts in order to implement demands of the respective constituencies. After all, they did provide the votes in exchange for what will shortly be exposed as empty promises. So, why not do a little something for them? They may require some reason to vote again. This requires deft agility in the give and take of skillful negotiating with other successful candidates.

Negotiating is a specialized sales pitch category all onto itself. It must be done in order to satisfy voters that something is actually getting done. Once again, this also must be perpetually undertaken while simultaneously re-implementing step one in order to maintain the cozy relationship with those much-needed voters.

Overtly it would seem that politics is nothing but a perpetual employment of superficial pitch, pitch, pitch. But alas, concealed deep within every political sales pitch there are subtle ambiguities that cloak the details in which the devil dwells. And from a politician, getting details out of the devil is infinitely more difficult than getting the devil out of the details. Governing people is a dirty sales pitch business, and with just a little research, one just might find a modicum of corruption residue concealed somewhere deep within the political process. In political parlance, governmental corruption is known as "politics as usual."

Political and law-based sales pitching generally results in our government's considerable contribution to, well, itself. There has always been a generally held mutual distrust of government, as well as a combined suspicion that, with a wink and a nudge, all of us are somehow being taken advantage of. I can offer no sales pitch that will alleviate this suspicion or, for that matter, any other skepticism you may have about our fine leaders.

Image vs. Substance and Philosophy vs. Pragmatism

In politics, image is a sales pitch, and image is paramount. It's infinitely more important than accomplishments. Accomplishments can be scrutinized, criticized, mis-characterized and disparaged by opponents. They can be an opponent's very source for defamatory rhetoric. Conversely, if an opponent's image is too harshly attacked, a candidate may risk exposing his or her own image to accusations of issue avoidance and shallow dogma. The power of image can either elevate or crush a candidate's possibility of success, unless it's powerfully and successfully sales-pitched.

In politics, a compelling sales pitch has the power to create and convey a commanding and authoritative image. A well-presented image-centered sales pitch can transform a negative perception into a positive opinion. An effective sales pitch doesn't change the candidate; it simply changes the image of the candidate. A politician who professes ideologies in specifics rather then generalities will never be as popular as a grand scheme generality candidate. Very few want involve themselves with the details. Voters just want a simplified promise.

Image and philosophical beliefs are what people can relate to and agree or disagree with. People are much more comfortable connecting with ideals than they are judging and analyzing issues. A politician's prowess lies in his or her ability to effectively present a favorable, advantageous, dominant and principled image: obviously while subtly and shrewdly exaggerating their substantive experience. Politics, my friend, is the essence of sales pitching popularity contest. A popular, well-liked candidate will almost always win over an accomplished but bland contender. What Politician has ever accomplished what their image conveys anyway?

Outward Appearance vs. Inner Workings

A brief bit of history here may be apropos. Back in the early seventies a tough and really smart woman was the chief lobbyist for International Telephone and Telegraph. (Back then it was one of the largest corporations in the world.) Her name was Dita Beard, and I will never forget her. She was dragged into the national spotlight during what can only be described as a turbulent period for then President Nixon and the Republican National Convention. According to the press, she had written an inner office memo linking the Nixon administration's settlement of an antitrust case against ITT with that company's illegal, quid pro quo contribution to the Republican National Convention. This was considered to be, in some ways, a prelude to the Watergate scandal.

As fate would have it, she was forced to stop in Colorado back in 1972 because of a sudden health issue. My father, a doctor, was contacted by one of his patients who happened to be a friend of Dita's. He was asked if it would be possible for him to visit her hotel room to diagnose her ailment. Unbeknown to my father, the entire national news media, not to mention half of congress, was on the lookout for her. It didn't take long for all of them to find out about my father's house call. No more than fifteen minutes after he returned home the phone rang. "Hello, this is the FBI. We need to speak to Dr. Garland." For the next few days our phone never stopped ringing. The months that followed were filled with shuttling her in and out of hospitals in order to facilitate some grueling congressional interrogations and visits from some colorfully costumed characters.

During the Watergate scandal that followed shortly after this fiasco we were watching the news at home. E. Howard Hunt, a prominent Watergate figure was being interviewed. My father laughed and said, "That's the guy who visited Dita late at night wearing a red clown wig, big glasses and a fake mustache." And you thought the people in politics weren't clowns.

When the dust finally settled and some degree of normalcy returned to her life she decided to stay in Denver. For the next few years Dita remained a patient of my father's and became a dear and very close friend of our entire family.

It was within this friendship that she divulged more than I can even remember about the true inner workings of our country's government. A good deal of it was pretty alarming and disturbing stuff. If her tales of behind the scenes governmental functioning taught me anything it was that John Q. Public is so far out of the loop of what actually goes on, that there's almost no way we can formulate informed, knowledgeable opinions regarding our leaders and what actually goes on in government.

As the "armchair experts" we are, all we really ever see or hear from the media or our other sources is an orchestrated sales pitch facade meant to comfort or placate us. In addition to being a wonderful and really intelligent human being, Dita was a genuinely tough and battle-tested old bird. She revealed to us through her accounts of firsthand experiential anecdotes the true sales pitch that is Washington DC.

Indecently, both direct and indirect ramifications related to that incident reverberate to this day. Legislation and Supreme Court decisions have been either an indirect result of or catalyst for legislation and Supreme Court decisions, e.g., the Tunney Act and the Citizens United ruling. Yes, times change but politicians are politicians. As tumultuous as those times were, they pale in comparison to the current climate of vile and contentious politics.

So, what are the inner workings and behind the scenes goings-on of our government? Only those buried deep within the bowels of our government really know.

All I can tell you is that if what you think you know came from the media, your friends or some supposedly well-connected grapevine, your knowledge isn't only profoundly deficient, it's totally lacking in credibility. Very few have legitimate or credible knowledge of what's really going on behind those marble columns.

People believe the political sales pitches that are comfortable for them to believe and castigate those who find comfort in opposing beliefs. I know it's absurd but in this world of alternative fact and fake news, we still lovingly refer to this as "politics as usual."

Dealing for Dollars

By whom and what are the three branches of our government driven, guided, directed and influenced? There are several answers, but some are more pervasive and persuasive than others. When I say our governmental branches are driven, guided, directed and influenced, I obviously mean, "sales-pitched." Other than the judicial branch, the most predominant tip of the influential spear is big money and those who have it. A great deal of money is required to both get elected and then stay elected. To a politician in the legislative branch, money is a spellbinding aphrodisiac, as well as an alluring taskmaster, especially when coupled with a large dose of self-serving motivation.

Most people are not aware that our federal legislators spend as much (or more) or their time fundraising as they do legislating. Aside from their fundraising, their big payoff comes when they retire into their respective reciprocal, bought and paid for, occupations. To say that legislators are not subtly, or even overtly, influenced and indebted to their sources of this money is naive and quixotic. If there were no returns on political investments, large donors would have little incentive to so generously participate. It's, indeed, an investment that expects returns. It's undeniably a monetary sales pitch carried out on a monumental scale. Aside from sex and fear, money is one of the oldest and most powerful sales pitches on earth. Ah, such is the price of power.

We all know that politicians need a whole bunch of money to get into the game and to stay in the game. Other than explicitly pleading for the paltry donations from individual mom and pop voters, how do you suppose they're able to acquire the massive amounts necessary to project their image? The word "reciprocity" pretty much sums it up. In a nutshell, this is one hypothetical example of how the sales pitches work in politics.

Let's give this scenario a try:

"We have a self-serving purpose and a whole bunch of money. We'll give you a large portion of our whole bunch of money if you espouse, advocate, promote and represent our purpose."

"Gee, I don't know, your proposition is

certainly a monetarily seductive sales pitch. You say that I can have this money for simply endorsing your purpose? Let me think now. Okay then, since I really do need it, I will accept a large portion of your whole bunch of money for promising to endorse and promote your purpose. But here's the thing, because I need to be seen as maintaining my principles, you must agree to express that you only gave me a large portion of your whole bunch of money because you bought into my sales pitch. A greed? Ah, sorry, I meant, agreed?"

"Absolutely. So, we both agree to your reciprocal participation for our monetary contribution?"

"Done deal. So where's the money?"

Pretty enticing sales pitch, isn't it? Money for power isn't only one of the oldest sales pitches, it's quite similar to sales pitches commonly associated with the world's oldest profession. Wait just a minute now, is there maybe some sort of connection here? Either way, I'm sure we all pay the price.

Many legislators have accepted funding only to become entangled in the puppet master's monetary strings. Influence and money are pretty much synonymous in the field of politics. At times, the very source of funding can expose a huge amount of truth about political intentions.

The Tea Party, for example, was touted as loosely organized grass-roots faction of the right wing. This is not unlike their left wing counterpart's short-lived "Occupy Wall Street" movement. The only difference is, if you follow the money, the Tea Party was hugely financed. I mean multi-millions by multi-billionaires, while the "Occupy Wall Street" movement, well, you know, fizzled into an unfunded pit of financial despair.

As viewed casually from the outside, it appeared that both were grass-root supported ideologies. In reality, the Tea Party gained most of its traction through backing from heavily financed sources. The sales pitch perpetuated fears of overreaching governmental controls. What do you suppose the results would have been if the Wall Street movement had received a benefactor's multimillion dollar backing and the Tea Party had only received the paltry, grass-roots monetary backing? That question was obviously rhetorical. Money can buy a lot of things, but more ominously, it can sales pitch a lot more.

Ah, but what about that Supreme Court? They have no financial skin in this game, and lobbyists never hassle them. So their involvement in political monetary distribution is a bit more nebulous. They are, however, no less immersed in the shenanigans of financial manipulation. While never personally financially benefiting, their political preferences and affiliations have certainly influenced decisions that ultimately resulted in significant economic impacts on the relationships between financial, corporate and governmental institutions. The first and most obvious example is the "Citizens United" decision.

With the Supreme Court's "Citizens United" ruling, the gates were opened wide for big money to roam free over the nation's political landscape and peddle its pitch to an already susceptible and gullible population. If you remember, the massive marketing and advertising industries wouldn't exist if they weren't so incredibly effective. So it goes with political influence.

The politicians who are backed by the most money will always have an edge when pushing agendas. They may not always win, but they will, without any doubt, have an edge. Over a hundred years of precedent gave way to the Supreme Court's "Citizens United" ruling. This ruling pretty much determined that corporate money has the same constitutional free speech rights as citizens. The results: influence can legally and anonymously be bought and paid for.

Was this the result of diligent constitutional interpretation or political bias? Either way, it certainly shifted the monetary structure of power. Take a real deep breath, exhale and, without choking, repeat after me; "Ahhh, there's nothing quite like defining which types of businesses constitute a citizen and which monetarily backed speech is free." (I still can't find exactly where the constitution references corporate rights, but I'm sure it's because I'm just not reading it right. I can never seem to find good old Jimmy Madison or little Tommy Jefferson when I need them)

Out in the Lobby

Money is indeed a powerful lobbyist. Financial reciprocity drives government as much as it drives big business and banking. Speaking of lobbyists, they are the representatives that industries, big business, banking interests, unions, gun advocates and a seemingly endless myriad of organization use to funnel their ideologies and influence and, yes, sometimes money to gain political access.

The steady rise of the lobbyists demonstrates the power of special interest sales pitching on a grand policy making scale. One might say that "lobbyists" are the grease that keeps the interconnecting gears of the big money machines and the government lubricated. And, because you read it in a civics book back in high school, you thought it was "we the people." Silly you.

Can you believe there are laws that were brought into existence through bills that most, if not all, of our elected federal legislators never even read? These bills were written by the industries that would benefit from the laws and presented by the lobbyists who represent these industries. It kind of makes the notion of "exactly who is running the country" a little foggy, doesn't it?

What, you didn't really believe that your senators and congressmen actually author these industry-affected bills did you? They don't have time for all that; they need to spend their time courting these industries and interest groups for reelection financing. It's a shame that "we the people" don't have powerful lobbyists.

Governmental Bent

Only slightly less influential than money is a strict allegiance and adherence to a political party. As just illustrated, the judicial branch is definitely included in this one. The subliminal obligations that are brought to bear by affiliation with party philosophies can be enormous motivators. The job of federal district courts and the Supreme Court is to impartially interpret the relevant laws and the Constitution then apply this interpretation to each case without bias. No matter how impartial they attempt to be, each Judge is susceptible to philosophical prejudices, even if it's subliminal or subconscious.

Because they are human, every decision they each make is influenced by these inherent prejudices. Their interpretations, however unwitting, are most certainly biased by their philosophical leanings. These philosophical leanings also encompass a bias toward the beliefs of one party or the other. The death of Supreme Court Justice Antonin Scalia certainly epitomized that.

It is humanly impossible to completely shut out personal bias in decision-making. Bias is an inherent characteristic of human nature. It can be traced back to a lifetime of experiential mental imprinting as well as our basic evolutionary group dependence paradigm and its relationship to comfort vs. discomfort.

This means that we find the ideology of one political philosophy more comfortable than another. This, in turn, makes us more vulnerable to the sales pitches of our preferred party. As a result, interpretation of the laws and legal decisions can be inadvertently, or even intentionally, influenced. So even those who reside over our courts, because they're human, are not immune to influences that are imposed by a political party. In politics, impartiality and neutrality are just words that mean: "I believe that it's in my best interest to never overtly divulge what I really believe."

The legislative branch is far more explicit in their display of overt, and, at times, belligerent, presentations of bias-driven agendas. Generally their beliefs are genuine and benevolent. After all, if it weren't at least somewhat genuine the sales pitch wouldn't ring true enough to get them elected. There is a requisite ideological transparency required to make a political sales pitch effective.

When all within a political party present a unified sales pitch, the party will be perceived to be stronger. However, there are circumstances where an entire congressional party can collectively find themselves victims of their own mutually agreed upon sales pitch. For example the Americans for Tax Reform organization's "No tax increase" contract was an extremely effective sales pitch. Taxes are uncomfortable, tax increases are undesirable and not increasing taxes keeps the constituents happy, so what's the question?

The answer goes back to the age-old argument of the government's efficiency and effectiveness at monetarily meeting the needs of the people. Fair enough argument, but in acquiescing to the conditions of a philosophically sales-pitched agreement, some politicians have subordinated their responsibilities to a non-elected author of this coercive extortion contract. Extortion? I'll leave that for you to decide. If they break from the agreement, the monetary interests behind the contract will redirect support to an alternative candidate who promises to remain a little more faithful to the cause. So those who don't live by the contract, die by the contract.

And now for the catch-22: as it turns out, adherence to this contract could severely limit the operational funding of the government. It's like a pre-teen signing a contract to never wear shoes any larger than the ones they have on now. Even pre-teens know that clipping toenails and removing socks would only work in the short term. Eventually, the toes will collectively demand a more accommodating increase in size. The downside for each of the participants in this contract is that their continued adherence to the contract could eventually cripple their ability to effectively function as a representative to their constituents.

Political Morality
How's that for an oxymoron heading?

Political morality is really a nebulous term that depicts a fictitious state of mind that's conveyed as an ideological reality for the purpose of sales pitching a nonexistent moral high ground to a mostly apathetic electorate in order to gain favor, or at least attention. The concept of political morality embodies a wistful expression of utopian ideals that are used as sales pitches to sway or assure the politically ignorant.

It's the politically ignorant who ultimately determines which one of the bozos we'll be ruled by. The rest are already polarized partisans and way beyond needing to be pitched. These devotees just need to be coddled. *Now, if we could only convince our leaders to follow, they'd lead us to where we all want to go: mostly away from all of them.*

The realm of politics is truly the definitive worldwide insincerity-laden sales pitch playground. Remember "institutional sales pitch deception" from back in the school chapters? Well this is much bigger and badder. As a matter of fact, it doesn't get any bigger or badder than government and the political sales pitches contained therein. The law, religion, business, and society in general all contain at least a modicum of hypocrisy and immorality. However, it is within the grand halls, columns and domes of politics that one can find the quintessence, the embodiment, nay the epitome of this "sales pitch" immorality. Now at some point in every person's life, they will lie to get something they want. With politicians it's a little different. In order to get what they want, they never quite get around to telling the whole truth. Most of the time all they really want is to get elected or re-elected.

Unsubstantiated accusations and unverifiable assertions are the bedrock of "fake news." Fake news is the instrument of choice in instilling fear or creating conflict. "The-sky-is-falling" fear mongering has been going on ever since Chicken Little ran against Foghorn Leghorn in the cartoon primaries. The press had a field day fact-checking the fowl opinions emanating from the spin rooms after that one.

Some cynics see government as a ruthless, egocentric megalomaniacal, but oh so inefficient, pinnacle of power and control. Others believe government to be the far too benevolent source of the citizenry's security and welfare as well as the prime protector of a communal social fabric. Other more realistic cynics believe that the government exists primarily to provide all of us with absolutely everything they can possibly take. This is a belief that pretty much applies universally to every form of government. If you aren't at least partially aware of the political mischiefs that a detailed analysis of any government would reveal, you must surely suspect.

One of the quotes attributed to Yogi Berra may be applicable here. "In theory there is no difference between theory and practice. In practice there is." In theory, every form of government on earth will function exactly as intended by its founders—unfortunately, in practice this condition cannot exist. Well, perhaps it could in a philosophical or idealistic vacuum where people are completely excluded from the equation. People have such a propensity to create rules that perpetually conflict with the rules that other people create.

Join the Party, Conquer and Divide, Leave No Middle Ground

A quick study of political "immorality" reveals a few basic types of marginally deceptive sales pitches. One plays on a portion of the population's inability to maintain a rational and unbiased level of objectivity. This type of sales pitch is almost a prerequisite for political public service. Unfortunately for the public, political viewpoints, as stated before, are born of a lifetime full of solidified bias and paid-for beliefs.

Embracing the comforts of a continual reinforcement of like-minded sales pitches renders the majority of politically engaged citizens almost completely void of objectivity and utterly incapable of impartiality. Radio and television talk, "news," shows exemplify this by dividing the nation into two "yup, he's right" herds of nodding heads that have almost completely abandoned all rational reasoning capabilities. I mean why would a proponent tune in every day simply to agree with all of these verbose mental manipulators without scrutinizing the veracity of their perpetually inane sales pitch babble? Well, maybe because it's genuinely comfortable consistently agreeing with these purported pundits. Besides, it allows them to have all of their analytical thought processes done for them.

Have you ever noticed that the conversations of both left wing and right wing zealots primarily involve complaints, accusations, criticisms and blame?

Almost all discussions are void of specific or realistic solutions. The emphasis here is on realistic. When a solution is introduced it's never discussed in terms of resulting ramifications. They stick to the safety net of a demeaning and damning use of criticism. That's why the "pundit show" airwaves are comprised of critics, accusers and illogical whiners rather than those who would present an impartial and balanced analysis. It's also why these shows all have a call screener. I mean you can't have callers asking questions that might require pragmatic, if obscure opposition-leaning solutions.

And still America listens on, perpetually acquiescing to the babble and nodding, as if some great truths have been revealed. This simply empowers all who listen with a reinforced prejudice and narrow-minded understanding of the objects of their own bias. After all, these gurus are only expressing what the listeners already believe. It's always so comforting when corroboration of our sacred opinions makes us even more right. My God we so totally smart.

Christening the Leader-Ship

Countries-governments-religion-organizations-clubs-organized groups, etc., all have leaders. How did these leaders become leaders? And why does most of humanity follow these leaders, regardless of truth, fact or reality? Well, its because we're all told to by the leaders.

When allegiance, compliance, obedience, conformity and loyalty reign supreme, are we following a sales pitch or our brains? Obviously we're following a sales pitch. Why? Because it's much easier and a lot more comfortable to believe or follow what another human thinks than to put out the effort it takes to think for ourselves. Or so I've been told by others. I really haven't taken the time or put out the effort it takes to think about it.

Most reasoning requires some effort. That's why most people do without it. When you accept the reasoning of another you allow yourself to forego the effort, time, stress and frustration that is often involved with being even just a little knowledgeably skeptical. You also relinquish any claim you may have had on being smarter or knowing more than some bozo you trust, respect or simply believe. Your thought processes and reasoning abilities atrophy just a bit each time you rely on the product of another's opinion or judgment. The faith you have in your own reasoning is slightly diminished each time you rely on the reasoning of others. If it weren't you would obviously be smarter and know more than they do.

The allocation of critical thinking and reasoning to another is the foundation that every system of government, every religion and, of course, every successful marriage is built on. Regardless of scale, the steadfast believers are generally the perpetual followers. True followers subordinate to another's position by accepting another's reasoning, logic or conclusions. Even to the degree of an insignificant point within the most infinitesimal facets of a discussion, followers remain loyal. Basing your own self-confidence on the un-scrutinized beliefs of others is lazy-brained self-deception. Just ask any ISIS member.

On a macro scale, the militant and fanatically obsessive "blind faith believers" are at the heart of religious extremism, fanatic terrorism and nationalist militarism. In a theocracy, religious zealots are sometimes the political parties that comprise entire theocratic populations. They depend largely on the strength and scope of the power of their leader. In some portions of the Middle East, there are leaders of rebellious followers and followers of rebellious leaders. Who is at the mercy of or in control of whom? In the US, aren't the leaders supposed to follow the desires of the followers when they become the leaders of the followers?

Why do you suppose it is that politicians, especially political candidates, never ever give a straight answer to a straight question? There are several reasons, of course, but the central theme to all of these reasons is that they have their own agenda.

A reliance on oversimplified generalities, elusive references, thought-provoking vagueness and purposeful ambiguity are the cornerstones of political survival. This is why a politician's answers are almost always either a restatement of the question in general terms that will vaguely satisfy their agenda or a general statement of their agenda regardless of the relevance to the question. I believe that specific answers by members of both political parties were barred by an act of congress somewhere around the time of the invention of recording devices. This was done to preserve the ambiguity of political integrity. The one exception to this rule is when a politician specifically and succinctly demeans the character of an opponent.

Politicians are all held captive by the promise of power through the righteousness of their own beliefs. They defend their self-justified beliefs with sales pitches that never waver, even in the face of reality. Unless, of course, doing so directly benefits them. One side theorizes that through hard work "anyone can succeed if they apply themselves." No they can't. Not only can't they but that statement defies logic.

To accurately assess the probabilities, one must first define what portion of the population "anyone" is and what constitutes success. Otherwise "anyone" is cumulatively everyone. We often hear the platitude: "If I can make it 'anyone' can." This is equally preposterous. This sales pitch presupposes that ability, capacity, intelligence level, circumstances and luck will all simply give way to effort and desire. There are some who mistakenly utilize this "hasty generalization" logic fallacy to argue that they do.

There are hundreds of millions in the category of "anyone" who, in spite of total effort, never succeed. For example, there are many who are capably or circumstantially unable to progress to a "successful" level. Barring an improbable wave of good fortune, an uneducated single mother of two who works at two jobs just to make ends meet is not going to "financially succeed." Yet the application of "anyone can" types of sales pitch are so effective they have become platitudes and cliché mainstays.

If we apply the same logic presented back in the "herd mentality" chapter to our extremely competitive population, we can identify most of the losers in our society. Some examples are: How many candidates generally ran for president last term? Now, how many candidates won the presidency? Just one. Simple logic dictates that all who did not win—lost.

By definition, losing makes them losers. The inference must be that if everyone who voted for the losers, by corollary association, are themselves losers. The logical deduction can only be that the world is primarily made up of losers. This conclusion is infinitely more valid than the statement that "anyone can make it."

On the far end of the opposing side of political ideology, a prevailing sales pitch theme is that there should be a very strong and all-inclusive, government provided, safety net. This takes "security" to a level of social and economic unfeasibility. This type of sales pitch totally disregards the pragmatic ramifications that personal economic incentives would be considerably diminished. It is assumptions like these that serve to destroy the credibility of a pitch.

If everyone were offered the security of food, shelter, clothing, transportation and healthcare without working or contributing to the economy, it would unquestionably motivate him or her to sit on their collective rear and collect.

The objective of providing personal security to all citizens, while honorably intended, has never proven to be plausible, sensible or realistic. By applying the same logic as above, the eventuality of such far-reaching policies would eventually produce a bankrupt, "do nothing" society. Where would businesses find a workforce in a population that makes more from government handouts than companies could afford to pay? Other than boredom or inner drive, what would motivate potential workers to even look for a job? Companies can't compete for workers in a "get paid for doing nothing" economy. But, in the end, it certainly is an attractive and effective sales pitch.

The arguments for both sides are so riddled with presuppositions and logic fallacies that a sales pitch representing either side as a realistic solution would be invalid and totally without merit. Yet both righties and lefties consistently fall for these sales pitches without any thought, examination or scrutiny. Ramifications of implementing these so called solutions are never even addressed. Why? Well, it's because most sales pitches don't point out the discomfort inherent in most sales pitch's presuppositions. Remember the comfort-discomfort paradigm? The involved application of critical analysis and unaddressed consequences can both produce discomfort. Sales pitches and discomfort seldom productively coexist.

Both sides provide compelling sales pitches that pander to those who want very much to have their own beliefs justified. Is there any wonder why such vile ideological conflicts exist? Diametrically opposed philosophies, like those illustrated above, present socio-political struggles that are almost impossible to reconcile. Unless, of course, a more persuasive and powerful sales pitch radically effects a change in the entire population's comfort level.

The only real cause for concern is that politicians on both sides are sometimes held captive by the compelling seduction of power and the righteousness of their own beliefs. They defend their self-justified beliefs with sales pitches that never waver, even in the face of reality, unless reality directly benefits them. Megalomaniacal-based sales pitches, when left unchallenged, can rapidly transform leaders into rulers. And if you missed it in your history class, the Revolutionary War was fought to get away from rulers.

We the People, the Wee People

I know how much you truly believe that your vote counts toward selecting our president. Unfortunately, when it comes to effectively affecting results, it's really just another sales pitch. Massive financial backing and the party leaders have either directly furnished the candidates or sales-pitched the delegates into selection capitulation.

So, regardless of your vote, the ones who you get to choose between are the candidates they have provided. Through a convoluted process of state-by-state primaries, caucuses and conventions, their candidate eventually emerges, and you haven't even voted yet. To add insult to injury, this candidate will always be answerable to the party and not to you. Unfortunately this leaves "We the people" as the only group without a perceptibly audible voice. Naysayers to this assertion will argue that your vote is your lobby. Seriously? This is our political system's dirty little "democracy"-based sales pitch to the citizens.

We, the voters, can only choose the "who." The "who" must be chosen from a group provided by the party's "who" providers. We produce the "who" by surrendering to the sales pitches that were bought and paid for by huge financial interests that hope to benefit from the "what" that their candidate may eventually provide in this reciprocity-marketing charade. The marketing of this "what" is, almost without exception, nothing more than a ruse or devious sales pitch. Most voters carry their vast array of preconceptions, biases and prejudices in the neck muscles of their dutiful and unquestioning nodding heads.

Did you ever notice that there are seldom any details or explanations of "how" the "what" is to be implemented? This never seems to be fully explained or even presented in a political campaign? The details of "how" are the most important aspects of a candidate's promised "what" intentions. If there is no "how" then the "what" is just a meaningless, empty, implausible platitude or undoable sales pitch.

"I will solve climate change, bestow financial stability to every citizen, resolve all world conflict and put an end to violent crime" is an example of rhetoric that's not all that dissimilar to the hollow promises that political campaigns are laden with. Why? Well, it's because releasing the details of "how" would expose the flaws in the capability to accomplish the "what." And that would most likely sink "who's" political chances. So, based on how susceptible we are to big dollar marketing strategies that provide us with their version of "what," our collective vote produces a "who." And regardless of how we vote, "who" will always win.

Hooray, it's "who" that finally gets elected. From this point on, either the "$" for "what" reciprocity obligation begins, or the inevitable lack of "how" creates a cluster of inactivity, or a never-ending flurry of finger-pointing deadlocks the works. Or better yet, everything moves forward through a massive nonpartisan cooperative effort. Yes, you are allowed to either wince or chuckle.

Is this a bit cynical? Well, yeah, but I'm certain that political history would be on my side. If you ever want to test the potential effectiveness of your "who," totally ignore the "what" and listen for the specifics of "how" in their campaign sales pitches.

It has been my experience that there are really only two things that the citizens would like from our government: transparency and accountability. These are really difficult to squeeze into a political sales pitch. The only way that citizens would ever get these is with a torture device. Politicians would never sacrifice both power and control by allowing the populous to know exactly who made which decisions and expose themselves to that kind of accountability. Power and control is why they are there. It is the nature of the beast that they would never jeopardize these marvelous weapons; er, ah, I mean these marvelous responsibilities.

So the reality is, whatever your political affiliation or philosophy you really have absolutely no influence or control, unless you are either adequately endowed monetarily or an active political participant perched on a really huge soapbox yelling into an exceedingly loud bullhorn.

If anyone needs a drink right about now, I think there's a couple of Kochs in the fridge. That should be enough to quench the political thirst of every man, woman and child attending their party. If you truly believe differently, you've been very artfully and effectively sales-pitched. (In spite of all of this, I still maintain my faith in the system and show it by casting my measly little vote. After all, someday it may actually count.)

That's Just What I Was Afraid Of
That good old "Weapons of mass destruction" sales pitch.

When it comes to dealing with the public, instilling fear and strategically utilizing that fear are the most effective sales pitch skills in a politician's arsenal. Connections, rhetorical skills, decision-making, planning, personality, negotiation and so forth, are all necessary abilities that leaders utilize when governing. None of these have the power to control the masses as effectively as the ability to create the conditions, or the illusions, that instill fear into the minds of the electorate.

Politicians have become adept at uniting the populace to a cause or ideology through the use of fear. And selling hope is so perfectly reinforced with an already effective implementation of a fear-based sales pitch. "If you're scared I am the one who can provide the security."

As was stated many times previously, "power" is the ability to deprive. If a population is presented with a situation or condition that may deprive them of any number of things, i.e., life, health, freedom, economic security, etc., the population becomes afraid and subsequently acquiesces to the security provided by the powers that be. The population relegates itself to a position of a dependent and fearing follower. They do this even if it sacrifices inherent constitutional freedoms.

When a population is threatened with losing the security that is beyond its ability to control, it rallies behind its leaders and gleefully bends to their reactive policies. Take 9/11 for example. Many policies were immediately put in place to mitigate the threat of another terrorist attack. Collectively we, the American citizens, were in fear of another attack. We certainly did not feel secure. Our fears were somewhat eased by newly adopted policies and procedures. Most would agree that these were probably necessary for our security. However, some argued that the continued addition of policies were actually infringing on our liberties and freedoms in the name of security. The possibility of losing some of these liberties and freedoms produced more fear in some than the fear of being terrorized.

The two conflicting political factions faced diametrically opposed fears: exposure to terror and loss of freedom. This duality diminished the power of the leaders and thus their control over the population. Even when the measures taken were successful, the fear continued. Why? Because, even if the most effective defensive measures are employed, most people are aware that terrorism will always exist in one form or another. Face it; it's been that way since Cain whacked Abel.

In retrospect, when analyzed within the realm of logic and reality, this excessive fear of falling victim to a terrorist attack within the borders of the United States is totally irrational. The probability of a terrorist significantly impacting even the most minuscule percentage of the US population is so minute that it is statically insignificant.

According to the CDC (Center for Disease Control) each year some 80,000 death are due to excessive alcohol consumption. If this is true, back on 9/11/2001, you would have been somewhere around 4700 times more likely to drink yourself to death than to die from a terrorist attack. Based on the number of attacks on our soil since then, the odds are astronomically larger than that. But terrorism pushes our emotional fear buttons and over-drinking does not.

Just driving a car presents a risk so much greater that, if scrutinized with the same application of fear, automobiles would be outlawed and highways would be closed. And yet "terrorism" is still the buzzword that drives the sales pitch that instills the fear that controls the population that follows the leaders that are protected by the fence that surrounds the house that Jack built.

It's not by accident that politicians, with more than just a little help from the media, tend to blow the risk of terrorism out of proportion. This generates the fear necessary to reinforce justification for additional measures that help them maintain control over the populace. If you doubt this just try sidestepping the TSA scanners prior to boarding your next flight.

Many would agree that we are slowly becoming a nation steeped in fear, all while being governed by those who would exploit these fears to gain more control. Removing our shoes at the airport never really made anyone feel safer. But have no fear, there will always be new fears to keep us paranoid.

We still have the fear of Mexican immigration, the fear of tax increases, the fear of talking to that really cute one and, of course, the fear of whatever the next topic is in the candidate's debate. (Or maybe even a justifiable fear of the candidates themselves) They do so look forward to pitching us on what to fear from the other candidate's position. These are the kind of pitches that keep the nighttime comedy show hosts perpetually supplied with sardonic fodder.

Liberal/Conservative, Right/Left, Progressive/ Conventional: Flip A Coin

Politically, our conflicting ideologies are really two sides of the same coin. Neither can ever seem to see the other side. Each side sales pitches a position they think represents the only valid and true value of the coin, and that the other side is worthless. Of course they're both wrong. Then again, they could both be right. Both sides of the coin could be steadily losing value. If we are lucky perhaps political inflation will eat away at the antagonistically based value of this coin. Or maybe each side will eventually devalue the entire coin to a point that renders it incapable of making the payment on our liberty and freedom. Only a flip of the coin will tell.

The following is a list of some of the more popular sales pitch techniques used by politicians:

- *Discretely plant seeds of doubt about the opposition's abilities.*
- *Always define the opposition and don't let them define you.*
- *Maintain a dismissive attitude toward an opponent's objections; avoid specifics at all costs, solutions are "generally" easier.*
- *Always rephrase questions to fit desired answers.*
- *Promise "blue sky"; hope is always a marketable commodity mis-characterize opposing beliefs.*
- *Plant conspiracy theories to evoke fear.*
- *Misrepresent the motivations or actions of opponents.*
- *Attack the opponent's character whenever possible.*
- *Be condescending to opponents whenever possible.*
- *Build up one's self by tearing the opponent down.*
- *Greet opposing views with mocking ridicule.*
- *Utilize "fake news"; the majority will believe it.*

The Law: A Universal Implicit Behavior Modification Tool

When the "law," the "lawmakers," "law enforcement" and the "courts" are all applied to interpretations of justice, what could possibly go wrong?

Once again, belief is one of the antonyms of fact. With this in mind, do you still believe that you actually know your rights?

"I am certain there are certain wrongs within certain interpretations of certain rights. I am also certain that I am right when I say that I may be wrong, at least with respect to certain rights."   I'm pretty certain this isn't quite right, right? What can I say? I mean, you know, without getting arrested.

Every law started out as a sales pitch. The first sales pitch for a law probably started out something like: "Everything would be fine if everyone could be made to just follow my rules." Others agreed, and poof, there was a law. Every law made since then has been initiated with pretty much the same sales pitch. Some alternative reiteration of "tha-oughta-be-ya-law" has been a perpetually repeated prelude to sales pitches for legal implementation ever since the word "law" came into existence.

An attempt will be made to exemplify the affects that sales pitches have on the underlying principles of "laws," and their origin, implementation and application. This makes it much easier to criticize the "law" in general through a few, more specific, sales pitch paradigms.

With apologies to those operating within the realm of business and/or sales, the field of law is truly a sterling example of convincing. Entire societies are forced to buy in. Laws have been authored and implemented by the forces of political leaders, wealthy autocrats, religious heads and military factions throughout the world. This alone should make most laws suspect. (In theocracies, religious leaders are the political leaders)

"Laws" aren't necessarily ethical or moral just because they're laws. Ethics and morals are in no way predetermined requisites of any law. At one time slavery was a widely accepted law of the land. Not a whole lot of moral or ethical grounds to that one. Yet it formed the basis of the most detrimental war this nation has ever faced.

Is it constitutional to pass a law that the courts interpret to be unconstitutional? If so, is that simply ignorance of the law, a law of the ignorant or simply ignorant interpretation? If ignorance of the law is no excuse, does that ignorance of the law preclude the necessity of the Supreme Court or a lower court whose ignorant ruling was appealed and overturned?

Are laws just some mildly effective instruments for behavior adjustment? No, they are society's definitive communal command structure for societal behavior modification. The laws themselves have never been proven to be universally effective deterrents to what the laws constitutes as crime. On the other hand, the fear of enforcement, adjudication and incarceration certainly has.

239

Few are sorry before getting caught. Almost everyone is sorry after being caught. Crime only pays when no perpetrator is caught. So obviously the implied sales pitch here is that there's only one law: Don't get caught.

Laws were originally created and enacted to protect human beings from being harmed by other human beings. It was learned early on that hurting people and taking their stuff isn't very nice. "Hey, don't hit your little brother and give him back his toy" is a modern family law version of this ancient application of societal law.

The application of law quickly began to encompass other protections. Laws were enacted to impose moral, ethical, philosophical, religious or other belief-based principles and protections. This served as an application of power and control. Regardless of how the position of "lawmaker" was attained, those allowed to author, enact and impose laws are, by the very nature of their position, imbued with the power to abuse these laws.

This is where the tricky part comes in. If they have the power to make, impose and enforce the laws, they are able to make laws that protect their position from those who might disagree and thus enhance their own position of power. Historically this unchecked application of law has lead to despotism. This is where the strong or violent rule over the weak and passive.

Where is the sales pitch, you may ask? Well, whole bunches of people had to either agree to accept, be forced to accept, or merely accept out of hand, the "lawmakers" and, consequently, the enactment and enforcement of their laws. Their position represents the culmination of some really serious and experiential sales pitching.

A Few of the Principles Behind Principled Laws:

1. *The Harm Principle: Laws that are written to protect people from being harmed by others. They include laws against violent crime and property.*

2. *The Parental Principle: Laws written to prohibit self-harm as well as to protect against neglect of children and vulnerable adults, and laws banning the possession of certain drugs.*

3. *The Morality Principle: These laws range from sexual behavior to hate speech and religious beliefs to personal morality.*

4. *The Donation Principle: Basically dealing with unjust use of favoritism from positions of power when used to control or reward behavior. They can give select individuals, groups, or organizations unfair advantages or, in alternative cases, punish or place undo restriction on others, all in an effort to leverage support.*

5. *The Statist Principle: These types of laws are intended to protect the government from harm, or, in more extreme cases, to increase its power for its own sake. This principle also encompasses laws that are against treason and espionage. The Statist Principle can also be abused. Laws restricting criticism of the government can lead to a politically oppressed society filled with citizens who are afraid to speak out.*

Little of this satisfactorily addresses human selfishness and individual craving for power and control over others. Lack of trust and dishonest people are the principal reason that laws are necessary to protect people. But how far can the law be trusted? It can only be trusted as far as unjust or abusive lawmakers can be thrown out of their position of power.

Using the Law for Gain: Legal Sales Pitching

Using eminent domain to displace thousands of long established residents for the benefit of private casino interests in Atlantic City. Enough said? No? Then how about extremely well-funded big guys lawfully forcing the hand of hopelessly underfunded little guys, e.g., when institutions, large corporations, employers with pricey law firms financially leverage to obviate an overmatched individual? Or how about simple predatory pricing to eliminate competition? Like a big box store displacing a community's small retailers by utilizing predatory pricing, and then, in cases where profitability doesn't meet corporate expectations of viability, leaving?

Even when David does triumph over Goliath, David is most often left debilitated. Legal inequity is sometimes a bitter sales pitch. There can be no level playing fields within unregulated "free enterprise" economies, where the free enterprisers are allowed to reciprocally finance the lawmakers.

Law Enforcement

There are times when law enforcement oversteps its authority or pushes the limit of its designated responsibilities, but that's relatively rare. We excuse most law enforcement abuses because without enforcement of the law—there is no law.

242

SECTION FOUR
The Warping, Twisting and Perverting
of Perceptions and Beliefs
{The Art Of Deception}

Chapter Eleven
– Self-Pitching –
It's A Real Son-Of-A-Pitch

Ever fallen in love? No, you didn't really fall, you simply, and quite gladly, submitted to your own emotional self-pitch.
And convincing yourself was all it took.

Inherited Genes Fit So Well, and They Hardly Ever Shrink

I have argued previously that our perception of reality is a jumbled combination of our genetics and a lifetime supply of sensory input. So now might be a good time to interject a little of our hereditary or genetic predisposition factor into the mix. Now, hereditary and genetic predispositions are really complicated biochemically integrated bunches of scientific issues that are definitely outside the purview of this little sales pitch subject analysis.

Suffice it to say, some of us are far more genetically predisposed to either pitching or falling for pitches than others. Basically our genetic makeup deals more with how our brains deal with sales pitches and self-pitches and not so much what we choose to buy into.

The method or process our brains use to interpret reality is, initially, more a result of our DNA. Heredity provides each of us with our own distinctive predisposed path on which the brain's activity leads our perceptions and interpretations. Yep, that means you have no one to blame but your parents. Everyone is screwed up to some degree, but each of us is screwed up in our very own unique and individual way.

Your parents have left you permanently burdened with your own personal genetic impairments, imperfections and deficiencies. It's their fault and there's nothing you can do about it. At least that's my sales pitch and I'm using it to get out of delving into a really complex biological subject that could make this book even more tedious than it has already been.

Wanting So Much to Keep Wanting So Much

The self-pitch progression commonly moves from "I see" to "I like" to "I want" to "I just gotta have" to "Okay, I got it, now what?" A large portion of our population actually grew up believing this is how they should acquire things. Aren't we a bunch of gullible suckers? The reasoning and logic we present to ourselves in a self-pitch isn't even that great of a sales pitch.

It's so simple. All we ever have to do is want. From that superficial motivation we can rationalize, justify and defend our willingness to buy into our own pitch without guilt or regret. The guilt and regret generally emerges shortly after we execute our buy-in. "Shortly after" is when we realize that our desires have taken advantage of our predisposed propensity to forego all rational reasoning. It's our punishment for being dumb enough to believe our own sales pitch. "Hey, all I did was want it—but I did want it real bad."

We're either really great "self-pitch" masters or guilty of habitual willful and purposeful convenient gullibility. Yup, most of us are nothing but gullible, self-placating suckers. We develop a tolerance and forgiveness through demented forms of self rationalized buyer's remorse. I have often found great comfort in forgiving myself for submitting to my own irrational self-pitches. Like most people, I am quite compassionate when it comes to me— and my gullible self-pitch acquiescence. I seem to be the only one with the capacity to continuously forgive "me" for whatever I talk myself into.

The parameters of positive motivations are based on the principle that we sort of want what we need, but what we really, really need is what we want. We need what we want because it's obviously more important than wanting what we need. Our self-imposed commitments to ourselves most often prevail over our externally imposed responsibilities and obligations. Once again, that's why we need, want and require a plethora of effective and well-tested excuses. Guilt-tripping, while effective, frequently gives way to "really, really wanting" what we want. This is akin to one of the reason guys want sports cars. Obviously the other reason is that they want to impress the really cute one. It's kind of a "two wants for the price of one" bonus.

The Inspiration to Be Inspired

Do people really need a coach, a trainer or a teacher in order to be encouraged? Motivation, whether positive or negative, is a sales pitch that people can, and do, effectively impose on themselves. Whether it's a kick in the rear or a grasp for the ring, motivation is a self-pitch that drives people in their pursuits. People push themselves in their pursuits for many reasons. And, more than likely, there is a sales pitch behind each and every one of these reasons, from a need to impress to an inherent competitive nature.

Many self-pitch motivations are inspired or provoked by outside sources. I often reflect back with a fond loathing to one of my particularly sadistic swim team coaches. I will never forget one of his clever little deceptions perpetrated to coax a self-pitch. During the week prior to a big tri-state meet we endured some particularly intense workouts. These workouts always culminated with timed sprints. We were all told to swim our hardest in order to provide our best time. On a couple of occasions, just after all energy had been expended to produce our best time, we were told we had to keep going until we beat that time. The self-pitch required to evoke enough motivation to accomplish that task was monumental.

This was the essence of utilizing a sales pitch to evoke a self-pitch in order to produce favorable results for both the pitcher and the self-pitcher. I'm pretty sure if you dig deep enough, you'll recognize that many of your motivations emanated from either an external inspiration or self-imposed obligation.

Friends and relatives employ various methods in sometimes innocuous or subliminal ways to provoke self-motivation. A parent may have been a successful athlete. Even without an overtly cajoling nudge, the inspiration to emulate can stimulate a desire. A more forceful or direct influence may drive the activity in a particular direction. "Guilt-tripping," for example, is one of the subtle but effective triggers used in these directing manipulations that stimulate self-pitching. "If you don't get back to your room and study you'll never be a doctor." The inference is that, "If you want us to be proud of you, you need to become a doctor." The resulting self-pitch would be, "If I don't get into that college, I'll be a failure and my life won't mean a thing." Or "I will disappoint my parents and they won't love me as much." These are just a few examples of the types of sales pitch sources that motivate personal pursuits.

Sometimes these sales pitch influences can even form the foundation of how and why people choose their direction in life. Whatever the source, whether explicit or subliminal, the sales pitches that we buy into push us or pull us in a direction we willingly go. "Willingly" is where a lot of our self-pitches reside.

Rationalizing Belief Justification and Justifying Belief Rationale

Do preconceptions cloud or bias any of your new observations or sensory inputs? Do you rely on your beliefs to shield yourself from alternative truths? Are you ever at odds with a bombardment of newly discovered "facts" or "truths"?

Whether you like it or not, the answer to all of these is, absolutely. If you objectively analyze your own beliefs you will certainly find that you have self-pitched them into infallible truths. What exactly is the basis or justification of those beliefs? Where did your beliefs come from? Did your conclusions lead to your beliefs, or did your beliefs lead to your conclusions? No human being is completely objective or totally without bias when assessing their self-pitched interpretation of reality. And believe me, people constantly delude themselves by warping their own interpretations of reality.

We convince ourselves the things we believe are not only truth and reality but significantly important. In both truth and reality, this is seldom the case. However, in order to maintain our sanity, we must believe they are. We do this through belief reinforcement self-pitches. It's just like the lion in The Wizard of Oz. "I do believe, I do believe, I do believe."

We all subconsciously (and even consciously at times) allow our beliefs to dictate, define and distort both facts and truths. Events of our past obviously effect our decisions and how we react to or deal with present situations. Successes and failures, accomplishments and squandered opportunities can and do influence or determine our reactions, responses and decisions.

Why? Evolution has provided us with a survival kit that includes some basic learn-from-experience skills. We have become somewhat dependent on these skills rather than rationally thinking, logically reasoning or solving problems independent of evolved responses. We convince ourselves that "been there, done that" applies to new circumstances, and no new thought processes needs to be applied. This sometimes results in what I call "lazy brain syndrome." I'm sure you've experienced this phenomenon—in others, of course.

So Many Convictions, So Little Judgmental Due Process

Don't be too concerned. Our belief paradigms and how they're affected by a stubborn reluctance to challenge pre-prejudiced perceptions are just our silly close-minded attitudes interfering with our rational thought process. With a simple, single-minded point of view—most people perpetually re-convince themselves that what they were convinced of was absolutely right. Reinforcing convictions seems to have escalated to epidemic proportions.

Never before in the history of the human race has each and every individual in an entire population been so convinced that his or her convictions are right and that everyone else's are wrong. Now what are the chances that everyone else is wrong? Now, what do you suppose the chances are that you're the only one who's absolutely right? Wrong, obviously I am the only one who is consistently right, except sometimes.

Beware the Placebo Effect

Have you ever tried to convince others that the pills you have are more than just benign sugar pills. By sugar pills, I mean wants and desires. Are you are driven by what you want, by what you think you want, what you think others want you to think you want or rather by what you are told to want? Are you really satisfied when your wants are satisfied? Except in the extremely short term, most people aren't. They simply move forward into wanting more. Thus this placebo effect is short-lived. Want satisfaction is a self-pitched promise of lasting gratification.

The panacea of want fulfillment is as hollow and ineffective as a sugar pill. Yet we perpetually pursue wants as if they are the cure-all that will eventually produce eternal comfort and pleasure. This is perhaps the most deceptive form of self-pitching. The probability that the Joneses, the ones who everyone wants to keep up with, are more comfortable or content than the rest of us is unlikely. The more stuff they have obligates them to a responsibility to maintain their cumulative advantage and position of envy. Just realizing that should make most people more comfortable.

So why do we collectively feel eternally driven and subconsciously obligated to keep up with those damn Joneses? Well, it's a complicated jumble of sales pitches, self-pitches and social obligation pitches. All of these pitches are placebo pitches. None of them deliver what they implicitly promise. The illusion that's created is status.

Remember status, the most expensive commodity on earth. It is really nothing more than an ego-driven display of one's desire to be seen as superior. This, in turn, manifests itself in a negative self-pitch based in the widely held self-perception that the rest of us are inferior. Since, in reality, we aren't inferior I guess this is what you could call a negative placebo effect. I know, I know, I'm just like you. I still really do want all that really cool stuff too.

A Matter of Interpreting Interpretations

When people see, feel, hear, smell or taste something, that's certainly not the end of it. I mean we're only human and human nature compels us to interpret it. What a strange bunch of curious, analytical and judgmental animals we are.

Reality is out there for sure. Even so, we humans pretty much see only what we want to see and hear only what we want to hear while discounting anything that contradicts our desires or beliefs? We identify intensely with that which reinforces our beliefs. We imbue ourselves with a unique ability to perceive only what we want to perceive. In short, we habitually convince (self-pitch) ourselves.

In psychology and cognitive science, it's referred to as confirmation bias, confirmatory bias or my-side bias. This is the tendency to search for, interpret, favor and recall information in a way that confirms our preexisting beliefs, all while giving disproportionately less consideration to alternative possibilities. It's why we hang on to our convictions, as though they are the foundations of our very existence.

Once you convince (self-pitch) yourself that what you believe is absolutely true, factual, correct, reasonable or justified, it's really tough to be "sales-pitched" into contradictory interpretations. Yes, you are both a victim and a prisoner of your own confirmation bias, i.e., the sales pitches you have previously bought into and become comfortable with.

It's far more comfortable to maintain favorable approval and reinforcement of your beliefs, as being accurate, than it is to question the possibility of alternative facts or truths. None of us want to admit to gullibility or that we sometimes forgo the application of rational thought to a sales pitch out of sheer laziness. It's so much easier to trust than it is to scrutinize or be skeptical.

Several studies on "event witnessing" revealed that most, if not all, ordinary folks self-convince. These studies start with an orchestrated event that is staged in front of a group of witnesses. The witnesses aren't informed of or aware of the experiment. After the event, each witness is independently questioned on several aspects of the event. Some of the questions are relevant to the action within the event others were relevant to the description of the people, their clothing and each of their specific roles in the event. Few, if any, of the witnesses accurately describe the details of the event.

This fact isn't as revealing as what happens when the group of witnesses is reassembled. During a group discussion it is found that people believe so much in their perceptions that heated disagreements break out over details as mundane as the color of a coat or the position of an object. Oftentimes, after reviewing a video of the event, several witnesses question the authenticity of the video, because it conflicts with their own closely held perceptions. Each witness is convinced their perception of the event more accurately matches all of the facts. Their beliefs are so firmly embedded they defend their own mistaken beliefs against the contrary, but also mistaken, beliefs of others in the group. Now how much do you trust the word of that bozo up on the witness stand?

Up until now everything your brain has amalgamated into is nothing more than a muddled pool of your tainted perceptions of facts. These perceptions have been filtered and refined into your notions, concepts and beliefs. All of these now fall into the realm of post-conceived. You know, "I don't care what the facts say, I know better because in my mind I have created a belief based reality that now trumps facts." If it weren't that way there would certainly be fewer disagreements.

Cling to your beliefs. That's it. Cling as tightly as you can because, after all, these are your very own dear and personal beliefs. You dreamed them up so they are a part of you. Don't fret. We all do this. But, are your resolute beliefs a result of your diligent thoughts or are your diligent thoughts a result of your resolute beliefs? I'm sure your self-pitch will clear it all up for you.

The more passionate you are about your beliefs the less someone else will be able to pry them from you. Yea, your values are strong, and you'd never let anyone sales pitch you into something contrary to your own self-pitched beliefs. Oh, hogwash.

You got your beliefs by picking and choosing from a laundry list of crap that's been steadily pitched to you. You have sorted through the info, the experiences, the teachings and the propaganda and chosen what's most comfortable for you to believe. Or you have chosen to align your beliefs with the beliefs of mentors, valued friends, respected associates or those with whom you wish to be accepted.

Your beliefs are made up of everything that conforms to the judgment system that you developed. Of course that judgment system is, as stated previously, almost completely based on your earlier set of beliefs. As a result, you are now saddled with the task of perpetually modifying, reconfirming, and thus solidifying, your own beliefs through self-pitching. We all strive to do this in order to satisfy our insatiable desire to, at some level, be right. I mean, really, who wants to be wrong all the time?

Some believe your true age can be determined by how long it takes you to get up off the ground without using your hands or arms. Actually, it can be better determined by how reluctant you are to alter, completely let go of or amend a steadfast belief. Beliefs seem to solidify with age. At some point they eventually progress to an irreversible condition where either "belief paralysis" or "rigor mortis of opinion" sets in. At that point even the best fact-based pitch-meister can't dislodge a belief.

So now begins the process of diluting yourself into believing, based on everything you have bought into throughout your life, that you are now "right." And, since you are "right," only those who believe as you do are "right." It also follows that, by exclusion, all who don't believe as you do are wrong. Of course this, by the universal modus ponens and modus talons rules of logic, means that everyone else who doesn't arrive at the same conclusions produced by your belief system is wrong. The problem is that beliefs, yours and everyone else's, are nothing more than solidified perceptions and judgments of interpreted facts and realities. They aren't facts and realities themselves. The world differs only in our perception of it.

Have you ever doubted something? Have you ever questioned the reliability of a source of information? Have you ever thought to yourself, That can't be right?

257

Of course you have. I mean just because everything out there is a sales pitch doesn't mean you have to buy 100 percent into it. You can, and do, constantly convince yourself. *Man, the best thing I ever did was to not listen to those jerks.*

Congratulations, you have just convinced yourself you're smart because you either did or didn't fall for a sales pitch. You have self-pitched yourself that, through the manipulation of your own brain patterns, that you made the right choice. You have given yourself the highest marks for a value judgment implementation. Okay then, if you're so smart, what was the ultimate source of the reasoning you used to arrive at this decision? Yes, you know where your reasoning source is. It's hiding in some manipulated minefield of memories from back somewhere in your past. A lot of these memories are booby-trapped with misinformation and bias. Just don't step on the wrong memory: it could destroy the entire basis of your decision.

As Luck Would Have It

Humans, by nature, really do want to believe in the worst way. And I do mean in the worst way. Admit it, even after being burned by a deceptive sales pitch you don't reject every proposition you're presented with. Lottery tickets still sell very well in spite of a never-ending series of losing numbers. We all unconsciously and instinctively maintain some optimistic desire to believe that we will eventually win.

Oftentimes luck is our only avenue to winning. Luck is a funny thing, sometimes just out of reach but still wholeheartedly believed in. All luck falls into one of two categories: good luck and bad luck. There are several kinds of luck within each of these categories. Each seems to be believed equally. Preparation-based luck, situational or circumstantial luck and accidental luck are some simple examples.

When preparation is successfully applied to an opportunity it's sometimes called luck. Thus the old adage, "Luck favors the prepared." If the star of the show breaks a leg falling off the stage, that's bad accidental luck. The well-prepared understudy is then presented with good situational luck as well as preparation-based luck.

Situational good luck can also be when someone is shot at ten times and every bullet misses. Situational bad luck is when one of the stray bullets hits a bystander. Accidental bad luck is when you crash your car. It is, by contrast, accidental good luck if you emerge totally uninjured. Regardless of the category or type of luck, we all sales pitch ourselves into believing, either optimistically or pessimistically, in some kind of luck.

Bernie Madoff made billions off this sort of blind optimism and a human propensity to really want to believe. Falling victim to deceptive sales pitches has burned even the most ardent cynics. People frequently buy into the sales pitches that prey on their preexisting desires. It's merely an enabling justification for guilt-free action. It is this self-pitched excuse your mind uses to justify your actions by holding an outside sales pitch responsible. I myself can validate or rationalize almost anything by blaming a sales pitch, even a sales pitch that I myself dreamed up.

Approving and Accepting a Perpetual Quest for Approval and Acceptance

More often than not, the more you try to impress others, the less you will, and the less you try to impress, the more you will. Why do we perpetually strive to impress others? Well, there's acceptance, approval, recognition, praise and, of course, the possibility of our own selfish pursuit of successful manipulation. It's kind of a self-pitch-based need born of a need-based self-pitch.

One of the most famous of all last words is "Hey guys, watch this." It is perhaps the most delusional self-pitches orchestrated in order to impress others with one's prowess. It generally occurs just before some catastrophic moronic, ill-fated stunt. The documentation of many of these can be found on social media Internet sites.

More rational forms of self-pitching present themselves in personal situations, environments or relationships; e.g., child and parent, employee and employer, player and coach, student and teacher, performer and audience and, of course, you and the really cute one.

It's generally not until we apply our early activities to life, that we realize the true benefits of aligning our self-pitches with those of others. "Okay now, don't fall," is usually the first self-satisfying instruction we receive when initially learning to accomplish an objective. We don't immediately realize how this benefits us, because all we do is repeatedly fall on our gushy diaper or on our face. Only later do we fully comprehend the joy and happiness that a sense of achievement can provide. We no longer impress others through successful exhibitionism. We impress ourselves. And it feels really good. These early "feel good" self-satisfying moments are the seeds that sew self-fulfilling self-pitches. Eventually we learn that accomplishing things purely for ourselves makes us really feel good, so we perpetually serve ourselves with pitches in an attempt to replicate the self-satisfying feelings.

There is, however, another side to this quest to self-pitch ourselves into acquisitions of comfort and happiness. It's the unfortunate adverse result brought on by not successfully accomplishing or acquiring what we have pitched ourselves to wanting. Nobody, not even a self-proclaimed failure, likes a failure. There are many options available to deal with "failure," i.e., keep trying, ignore and move on, alter expectations, analyze and adjust the effort, and so on. Nobody gets everything they pitch themselves into wanting.

When "not accomplishing" is pervasive and persistent enough, it can eventually evolve into a capitulation to a desire to give up or never try, which can lead to habitual despair and even depression. The self-pitch then becomes, "Why try when all I do is fail?" This almost always results in a quest for an alternative comfort that involves some form of escape.

Coping mechanisms of escape range from perpetually doing nothing to drinking, drugs and even suicide. For many people it is difficult to understand the tobacco, alcohol and drug industries thrive simply because so many people seek their products for the relief or escape from the agony of failure. These industries prosper because so many have self-pitched themselves into surrendering to their inability to successfully accomplish or overcome adversity.

Suicide hot-lines proliferate for the same reason. Suicide is often the result of anticipation that there is more comfort in dying than there is in living on to fail again. Some forms of depression are the result of perpetually feeling this way without actually resorting to the act.

Phobias, Superstitions, Ghosts and Other Irrational Self-pitches

A majority of the US population actually has a greater fear of public speaking than they do of dying. Perhaps it's jealousy that allows us to admire political speakers for their outspoken distinctive courage even though we may hate them for the words they speak.

Ah, the paradox of the love/hate political profundity we sell ourselves on. The question here is, are phobias congenital, self-pitched or a result of externally imposed circumstance or experience? The answer is yes.

The reason public speaking was illustrated here is that it is one our strongest and most common phobia. Why would the majority of a free society's population convince themselves that public speaking is such a horrifying experience? Is it a fear of failure, fear of looking stupid, fear of personal exposure, fear of ridicule, or maybe even fear of not being able to envision the audience naked? Whatever the reason, an irrational fear is at its core.

Whether verbal or physical sign language, most people in America, over a certain age, can speak. Almost everyone can stand in front of a bunch of people. Why is it that so few can comfortably do both simultaneously? Do we all suffer from some form of anxiety disorder? No, not really. What we have done is convince ourselves that there is an extreme discomfort associated with exposing ourselves to the embarrassment of public scrutiny. Rationally, there is very little downside to public speaking. Other than espousing some bizarre threat or inflammatory prejudice what negative impact could there be? Other than the possible discomfort of a little embarrassment, there really is no downside.

The consequence of a poor speech performance is totally introspective. Translation: Most people have self-pitched themselves into a belief that massive discomfort overwhelms any possibility of comfort that may be gained from public speaking. We have convinced ourselves that any situation providing nothing but discomfort should not only be avoided, it should be feared. Once again self-pitching the irrational trumps the rational. Self-imposed beliefs overwhelm realities.

This fear-based paradigm is a basic characteristic that's common to most phobias and superstitions. The subject of ghosts and spirits, on the other hand, deals with the possibility that whatever we sense but can't see, hear or feel is a major force that we truly need to fear. In essence, we—inherently or circumstantially—self-pitch ourselves into fearing whatever isn't out there.

Fear of the unknown has existed since the beginning of man (and woman). The source of this fear of the unknown is not unknown. It's a subconscious survival instinct. It goes clear back to our primal "survival of the smartest" evolutionary trial and error paradigm. It's the old "positive/false positive - negative/false negative" reality survival test.

To illustrate our human origins of this dilemma, may I present a potentially deadly quandary faced by one of our earliest ancestors? A primitive man, alone in clearing, hears a rustling in the surrounding tall grass. This rustling could be caused by one of only a few things. It could be a breeze, fellow tribesman, a hostile enemy tribesman or a carnivorous predatory animal. That works out to be threat assessment of just about 50 percent.

Now, since this guy had recently lost one of his buddies to whatever made the rustling last time, he is a little apprehensive. He has learned that not getting killed or eaten would ultimately work out better for him. Being prepared for the worst is, therefore, the best response, regardless of which of the four possibilities is presented.

Ever has been the resulting inherent human condition: fear of the unknown. Darkness seems to suffice as the current tall grass substitute. As for the monster in your closet or under your bed, I can't really help you there.

The Self-Fulfilling Prophecy

A self-fulfilling prophecy is when the belief in a prediction becomes so great that all actions taken are designed to produce an outcome that satisfies the prediction. A prophecy is simply a fixated focus driving an irrational premise directed at pursuing a belief-based prediction. If the conditions for fulfillment of that prediction are orchestrated to produce the desired outcome, the prediction is seen as satisfying itself, i.e., "self-fulfilling prophecy."

Allow me to set you up as an unsuspecting patsy. Even though you have done nothing wrong a cop arrests you. The cop convinces other cops of your guilt by simply spreading the word that he is 100 percent positive you're the guilty party. Based on his conjecture they collectively embark on an evidence-gathering crusade that, from the start, is focused only on evidence that would support your guilt, i.e., the prophecy. Interviews with friends and coworkers are conducted with questions that are laden with preconceptions or presuppositions that, when edited to their purpose, can be used to reinforce the suggestion of your guilt. After you are convicted and sentenced, you have lots of time to contemplate the power of a sales pitch born of this cop's "self-fulfilling prophecy" of which you became a victim.

This happens all the time with corporations or industries monetarily sponsoring studies that seek results that are favorable to them. Somehow, almost mysteriously, the results of the vast majority of studies that are heavily funded produce findings that are in the best interest of those doing the funding. Didn't you find it a bit curious that the results of some really well-funded studies revealed the relationship between cigarette smoking and cancer was non-existent? If you need an example of self-pitching on a massive industrial level, this, my friend, is it.

So, the sales pitch message here is that if you want to prove something bad enough you can set up circumstances that will allow you to do it. If you truly want something bad enough, you must actually sales pitch yourself into acting on what may be a really frenzied irrational desire.

Fortunately, there is also a positive flip-side to this phenomenon. Almost all successful athletes utilize visualization techniques to prepare themselves for their predicted results.

Visualization is a personalized attempt at a self-fulfilling prophecy. Professional golfers present a perfect example. Prior to actually striking the ball they visualize themselves utilizing the perfect swing required to hit a perfect shot that will result in a desired outcome. This reinforces the ability to effectively achieve their objective. The "prophecy" is a predicted successful result. The "self-fulfilling" part lies in the relationship between the preparation and a successful execution that visualization provides.

Business people accomplish the same thing through diligent planning and implementation of well thought out expectations of the results. Visualization has been proven to be one of the most effective and successful self-pitch exercises. At least that's how I visualize the successful conveyance of what I just presented.

Motivation, Desire and the Lack Thereof

An enabling drive for success and a disabling fear of failure are opposing forms of their respective inspirational and restraining self-pitches. They are self-imposed empowerments and restraints. "I can" and "I will" are incredibly forceful and enabling self-pitches that can drive individuals well beyond their perceived limitations and, in exceptional cases, their inherent capabilities. (*Isn't adrenaline wonderful?*) Inversely, "I can't" is a debilitating self-pitch that can render self-disbelievers functionally incapacitated, self-sabotaged and personally despondent. Both of these enabling and disabling scenarios are forms of self-deception self-pitching.

Humans do have an inherent tendency to self-deceive themselves. A great deal of human self-deception is negative. Negative self-deception is a disabling form of self-pitch. Self-imposed disincentive and restrictive parameters serve as convenient excuses to relieve us of responsibilities or obligations. Rationalization is a similar self-pitch that allows for evading or avoiding unwanted external commitments. As a matter of fact, we all have our own personal arsenal of excuse-based "I really don't want to" self-pitch justifications. These are truly the disenchanting tools that enhance our motivation to be unmotivated.

The Power of Perceived Credibility

There are instances when people purposely, arrogantly or even insentiently self-pitch themselves into the realm of superiority. Unfortunately, this groundless credibility can produce a pretty offensive sense of self-righteousness. What, you've never known anyone like this? If not, you certainly don't know many people. The self-important empowerment produced by even pretending to know more or have more power than another can become intoxicating to some.

When this illusion of power or self-image of knowledgeable superiority is baseless it imparts a subconscious manifestation of self-imposed authority. *It also generates repulsive and hostile reactions from everyone else.* Yes, it's a false power, but the power is felt all the same. The sales pitches that emanate from this condition, while unfounded, can and oftentimes do command power and influence over others. This is the power of perceived credibility and is commonly displayed by bullies, politicians and pompous celebrities.

The volatile mixture of ego, authority and perceived or faux credibility can wreak havoc on truth and reality. Stock analysts, movie, theatrical, book and art critics accompanied by a variety of other, so called, experts often share the same lack of genuine expertise. There is a formidable reliance on the assumption of credibility at play here. A stockbroker, for example, has no more ability to predict the future performance of a stock than you or I do, unless, of course, they are an insider trader. Yet, because they've passed a series of credibility-producing qualification exams, they're perpetually relied on for advice in choosing stock investments.

Then there are the old mental facility studies, where sane people were brought in for evaluation. This is where professional bias clashes with, and is compromised by, presupposition.

Now why do you suppose it is that these professionals would determine that perfectly normal people would be in need of psychiatric care? In short, the presupposition is that if someone is brought to the nuthouse, they must be nuts. All the doctors have to do is justify this through their infallible credibility. Of course this credibility is accompanied by simple presupposition followed by a requisite self-fulfilling prophecy.

These professionals have risen to a position that allows them to sales pitch themselves into a delusion of infallibility. Self-perception turns to self-deception with a simple self-serving sales pitch. This effect can be exaggerated even further. The implementation of questions that are prejudiced toward a desired response along with selective interpretations of the answers are all that's needed to achieve the desired, pre-determined results.

It's pretty much the same for medical specialists in other areas of medicine as well. Whatever the malady, it will be scrutinized from the viewpoint of their specific field. A simple backache can be diagnosed as kidney problem by the internist, a spinal problem by the orthopedic or a posture problem by the osteopath. Even a podiatrist can sell you a special $250 insole that will most certainly take care of that back problem. Each will have a remedy based on their specialty, which may or may not be the accurate diagnosis that will ultimately provide the remedy. And because not too many insurers cover that all-important second opinion, few are ever pursued. Makes you think twice about going to a specialist, doesn't it? Every profession has its self-serving beacons of self-pitched credibility.

Entertainment critics are an example of misplaced "perceived credibility." How many movie critics have ever been asked, invited or recruited to write, produce, direct or star in a major motion picture? None? Well maybe their personal contribution to any movie they pretentiously endeavored to criticize is a testament to their true motion picture industry credibility.

With regards to self-pitching, these immortal words of Abraham Lincoln pretty much epitomize their effect: "Most people are about as happy as they make up their minds to be."

Chapter Twelve
– The Magician's Tent –
(Where Deceptions Proliferate and Illusions Are Presented as Reality)

This is where misinterpretation born of misdirection, alteration or distortion of sensory input, and other psychological and physiological BS reside.

Magic: The Reality of Illusion, and Our Illusions of Reality

When we rely on our sensory observations to let us know what's true and what's real we can sometimes be, and often are, duped. There have been philosophical speculations that reality may not even exist. In an unprejudiced search for truth, Descartes, a famous philosopher, articulated reasoning that pretty much countered that notion. Incidentally, "I think, therefore I am," is a misquote that has been attributed to him.

His actual revelation was based on an effort to reduce everything to an absolute truth through the proposition that the existence of anything or everything could be doubted or denied. He could not, however, doubt or deny that he was, "in reality," doubting and denying. Since he was, in reality, doubting, he must, in reality, exist. So his initial conclusion was more like, "I doubt, therefore I exist." The mere act of doubting verified and validated his existence. It was an irrefutable proof that couldn't be doubted or denied.

Nevertheless, in the interest of a more coherent and practical approach (if there is such a thing), we will stick with the more traditional versions of reality. That said, it's sensory input that serves as the conduit through which reality gets conveyed to the brain. The brain then perceives this reality and stores it away in its cerebral warehouse of mental perceptions. As far as the brain is concerned, these perceptions are tied directly to realities and are therefore assumed to be the same thing. Au contraire, mon frère. The brain is wrong. Think "magic." No, not real magic. I'm talking about the theatrical illusion kind. Real magic is when a loved one forgives you for being a jerk or when your child does what you ask without complaining or wanting something.

An example of illusionary magic would be when the brain perceives that a live bunny is, in reality, pulled out of what that same brain perceives to be, in reality, an empty top hat. How is the brain going to deal with these conflicting realities? It doesn't have to. There are no conflicting realities. The brain only has to deal with conflicting perceptions. The empty hat is a reality. The bunny being pulled out of the same hat is a reality. A real bunny being pulled out of a real "empty" hat is merely a flawed perception. The illusion is simply the brain's mental perception sales pitch. A misinterpretation of sensory input can sometimes render a brain vulnerable.

There is always room for some degree of unreliable mental interpretation. Everyone is susceptible to the reality of illusions and the illusionary magic that is a fundamental ingredient in most sales pitches. Otherwise said, the brain's awareness of reality is not reality. It's merely a vulnerable perception. If you aren't convinced, then my magic is obviously not working.

The Other Alternative Reality

Several subjects, who were unfamiliar with the concept of virtual reality, took part in an informal experiential experiment. They were brought into a room and instructed to put on virtual reality visors. These visors were connected to a computer. (In addition to consumer applications, many college and professional sports teams use these for reaction training.) The computer was set up to generate a virtual scene in the visor. The scene in the visor mimicked the physical movements of the subject wearing the visor to simulate an accurate perception of reality. The virtual image each subject experienced was of the same room but with a wide gaping chasm in the floor.

A narrow wooden plank spanned the open pit connecting one side of the floor to the other. The open pit appeared to be either very deep or completely bottomless. Each subject was told to first bend over the edge of the void and look into the chasm. When doing so, each subject showed signs of being a little uneasy. They were then told to step onto the narrow plank. A couple of the subjects were so uncomfortable with this they refused to take a step. The ones who took the step were told to actually walk completely across the void on the plank. The few who did so proceeded with such extreme caution that it resembled a high-wire act.

It should again be stated here that every one of these subjects was fully aware they were in a normal room. They had been brought into the room prior to putting on the virtual reality visor. They knew the reality of a solid floor.

Why then were their reactions so dramatic? It was because their brains had been sales-pitched by the sensory image sent by their eyes. So convincing was the visual sales pitch that, even when armed with the knowledge of reality, their brains perceived the same danger that their eyes perceived. They didn't fall off of the plank; they fell for the virtual perception of a self-pitched reality.

Such is the deceptive sales pitch effect your senses can have on your brain. Your personal reality is, in reality, nothing more than a perception that your brain has been sales-pitched into interpreting as reality. A brain's interpretations simply validate perceptions of reality whether real or not. Remember, it's the conception of a deception within a perception that invites reception of the inception of a misconception.

Deception

Ever been deceived into doing something you didn't want to do? Ever had justifiable buyer's remorse? Ever been made to feel foolish or embarrassed? Ever unwittingly done something really stupid? If you have never experienced any of these, please, gently place this book on the ground and walk away. You aren't human and you are not of this earth.

If you have experienced any of these, pretty much like every other human being on the planet, you've been deceived. There are a multitude of victimization sales pitches that people endure every day. We have all been on the receiving end of these types of sales pitches.

Even a simple bet can be a form of deceptive sales pitch manipulation. My college roommate made use of an even more deceptive sales pitch bet. He would make a bet that he knew he would lose. It would be a bet with a girl he would like to take out. The conditions were that if he won she would have to buy him dinner. If she won he would have to buy her dinner. No matter who won, she would have to go out with him. This type of deceptive sales pitch is totally about getting what you want by trickery. Unfortunately for the girls, this almost always worked.

Deception wears many facades, but all deceptions, even self-deceptions, are sales pitches. Being set up as the villain while being told you are the hero, wrong presented as right, evil presented as good, the Trojan horse, believing warped mirrors accurately reflect reality are but a few of the numerous types of deceptive sales pitches. Intellect, logic and skepticism are not always sharp enough tools to cut through all of the deception we encounter. But without these tools we become gullible, reliant on blind faith, submissive to distortions of truth and reality and are frequently deceived with partial or misrepresented facts or realities.

When a perceived fact or reality is revealed to be an illusion or falsity it leaves us with only our beliefs to depend on. The problem is our beliefs are tainted by subconsciously concealed or repressed deceptions that our former self has never let go of. When a person is unwittingly deceived into a belief that is without basis in fact or truth, he or she will still defend it as a fact or truth. Why? Because it has been BS filtered and now resides in the domain of their personal belief system and must be treated as truth until discredited.

Within the context of manipulation, deception can easily be utilized to falsely lead others to believe that bad is good or wrong is right. Concealing truth has always been a pretty common human practice, i.e., *the Trojan horse, reaching an orgasm, the ingredients in a hot dog. Need I say more?*

Using the illusion of truth can lead to delusions and mistaken or flawed conclusions. They can also set up mischievous deceptions. Your memory probably just flashed back to some former jerky classmate whose pranks or practical jokes were almost constant sources of irritation to everyone. Pranks and practical jokes generally involve a misdirection of attention in order to perpetrate that all important "gotcha" moment. Yes, deception is often really annoying.

There's not a brain out there that can't be tricked by another brain. As a mater of fact, the more receptive a brain is, the more susceptible it is to being tricked. Sight, hearing, touch, smell and taste are the only informational pathways to the brain, and every one of them is susceptible to deception.

A sinister type of deception was utilized many years before virtual reality technology had been invented. A torture technique employed sensory manipulation to alter perceptions of reality in order to gain information. A prisoner would be secured in a chair. A small caldron of red-hot burning embers would be placed in very close proximity to the prisoner. The smell and the heat would permeate the room. Splattering a couple drops of water on the embers would then produce an intense sizzling sound. While still exposed to these sensory stimulants, the prisoner would be blindfolded. His arm would be forced into a position where his hand could be put into the coals.

Unbeknown to the prisoner, the caldron with the embers would be moved just enough to facilitate replacement by a large bowl filled with crushed ice and water. The interrogation torture would involve plunging the prisoner's hand into the ice. The prisoner, of course, believed his hand was being burned to the bone. This type of torture was utilized to protect the torturers from legal scrutiny that any visible physical wounds would leave them accountable. It's my understanding this was a very effective interrogation technique. Having never been burned, the prisoner never showed any signs of abuse, and thus, any claims of torture couldn't be proven. Was the burning a reality? Of course not, except, of course, to the prisoner.

Deception is one of the better sales pitch tools that mankind ever came up with. Even if it's to the smallest degree, everyone lies, everyone cheats and everyone deceives. At some point in her life I'm sure that even Mother Teresa was guilty of some innocent infractions.

There are so many kinds of lies that sometimes people lie without even knowing they've lied. It's pretty much been that way since the cave man. I can only imagine the cave man's version of this distraction type of lie. The, "Wow, isn't she a babe?" distraction employed in order to sneak a quick, unseen bite of whatever they killed that day.

This isn't unlike the universal modern day diversion tactic utilized to snatch a couple of french-fries from a buddy. Was it really a lie? After all, maybe she was a babe. No, the lie usually lies in the hiding of the truth. "Look over there, so I can steal a couple of your fries" would have been the truth. The lie is in the deception and the deception is in the lie. Distorting the truth even a little still results in distorted truths, and aren't distorted truth really lies? Do lies that are never revealed as lies live on forever as truths?

Conditioning a Response with Faulty Logic Fallacies

Fallacies constitute the Slippery Slope of a Red Herring in the Hasty Generalization of a False Dichotomy in every Straw Man Argument.

Listed here are just a few of the many types of faulty logic fallacies found in the specious sales pitch tool chest that are often utilized in winning arguments and influencing people:

A Red Herring is a fallacy in which an irrelevant topic is presented in order to divert attention from the original issue. "Yeah, I know this spinach is good for me, but I'm not going to eat it because I'm really tired and I think a little rest would make me feel much better."

The Slippery Slope is a fallacy in which a person asserts that some event must inevitably follow from another without any argument for the inevitability of the event in question. "We have to stop the tax increase! The next thing you know, they'll be taking all of our income!"

Ad Hominem is an attack upon an opponent in order to discredit their argument or opinion. "He's nothing but a wacko from Hollywood. He'll never know what New Yorkers want."

The Straw Man fallacy *involves misrepresenting or exaggerating an opponent's position to make it easier to refute. "Gun owners should take gun safety courses." Refuted with, "Any imposed requirements for gun ownership are a restriction of our second amendment rights."*

Ad Ignorantiam *(or **"appeal to ignorance"**) is the fallacy that a proposition is true simply on the basis that it hasn't been proven false or that it is false just because it hasn't been proven true. "He is obviously guilty because he didn't prove his innocence."*

Ad Populum *is the bandwagon argument fallacy. If everyone is doing it, it's not only acceptable, but it's preferable, and sometimes even customary. "But, officer, everyone was going that fast," or "If most people believe it, it must be true."*

Argument from Authority *is the presumption of expertise or knowledge that leads to, or serves as the basis of the acceptance of a conclusion. "George knows what you did was illegal. He knows the law because he played a judge in an Academy Award-winning movie."*

Hasty Generalization *is where conclusions are based on insufficient or unrepresentative evidence. "The kitchen light doesn't work. The electricity to the house must be out."*

False Dilemma *is an assertion that implies that there are only two options when, in reality, there may be many. "She has two ex-husbands, so her car had to be stolen by one of them."*

Begging the Question *(otherwise known as **Circular Reasoning**) is where evidence believability depends on the believability of the claim, or an attempt to prove a proposition-based purely on evidence that lacks its own proof. The Bible tells us that God exists. We know this to be true because God wrote the Bible.*

280

There's almost no limit to the ways that logic and reason can be perverted or contorted for the purpose of eliciting a buy-in to a deceptive sales pitch.

Warped Manipulation: How to Build Metaphorical Distorted Carnival Mirrors

Deception, criminal intent, threat of force, brainwashing, guilt-tripping, obligation, embarrassment, humiliation or just plain old trick-or-treat are all manipulative techniques used to bend you to their will. Talk about malicious sales pitches.

An example that's simple and less overtly sinister: *Promises,* those nebulous sales pitches that progress with only vague accountability—*also refer back to Chapter Eleven on political morality.* A promise isn't a guarantee. It's not a binding contract. A promise is not even a commitment. It's a sales pitch.

It is a self-imposed unenforceable obligation of will or intent, i.e., "I promise this will be your favorite book." A conditional promise is the sales pitch version of a regular promise. "If you buy this book, I promise it will be your favorite." In order for my promise to be fulfilled you must first buy this book. This is obviously a sales pitch promise. "Trust me" is usually an equivalent form of this kind of promise. Indecently, lies are really just dishonest promises of truth. You can be assured of this by my promise that these assertions are absolutely true. "Trust me."

The Sales Pitch with a Subtle Disguise
Manipulation through deception and deception through manipulation

We've all seen the expiration dates on our food goods. Why are they there? Did the FDA mandate expiration dates? Except for infant formula, product-dating isn't a federally required or regulated obligation. These dates were originally brought about either by pressure from consumer groups or, as legend has it, by Al Capone. (This is an assertion that may actually be true.)

Nevertheless, manufacturers grabbed onto this moneymaking opportunity before it had a chance to expire. If you look closely at various products, even some of the same products, you will find several versions of "expiration." There are "use by," "sell by," use before and even "best by." These are all pretty much arbitrary dates. They are determined entirely by the manufacturer.

Now, since profit is usually the primary objective of most companies, they would like for you to buy their goodies more often than you really need to. So, in the interest of increasing their sales volume, they use these dates to inform you that you need to throw the old one out and buy another one. The insinuation is that since the one you still have in your fridge or cupboard is past the date it might not be healthy. Well, not so fast there partner. It's been proven that the vast majority of "expired" products remain healthy and flavorful well past the expiration date. And yes, in a large number of cases, even milk is fine. Your nose and eyes are often better indicators than the dates on the labels. I mean if that fuzzy green stuff is starting to show on your bread and processed cheese product, it's probably not the best time for grilled cheese sandwiches.

Expiration dates are seldom a valid toss out signal. Even though we might be armed with this knowledge, most of us are still unwilling to take the risk that was planted in our brain by the food suppliers. Food shoppers of America have been sales-pitched into being vulnerable insecure cowards, and I admit to being one of them.

A sales pitch subtly disguised as caring about someone, or how to start a non-relationship for the purpose of personal fulfillment. Okay, now we're back to "the line." You want something from someone. How are you going to get it? You don't even know them. Whether initiated by a formal introduction or a self-asserted personal intrusion, the "line" is almost an indispensable necessity.

The most effective sales pitch strategy is to maintain the conversational focus on the intended subject. Nobody wants to hear about you anyway. One of the most successful techniques in successful opening conversational sales pitches is this questioning ploy. The decoded version of this is: *"Tell me what it is that you want to hear, and I'll tell you exactly what you want to hear."* This is not only the basis of initial relationship manipulation; it's the basis of most effective sales pitches.

The Pied Piper's Tunes Are So Easy to Follow

Grifters and con artists will present you with exactly what you want to hear, see and believe simply to benefit from the deception. They can skillfully persuade you to misconceive what you perceive into whatever it is they want you to believe. Then they deceive you into benefiting them by fulfilling a need for something they made you believe you should receive. If they're really good, you won't even perceive what they did to deceive you.

Fact or fiction, reality or fantasy, truth or illusion, the choice is yours. But you do have a choice. That choice isn't only based on what you perceive and what you believe but also on what you believe you perceive. (Sounds a little like the preamble of an old Moody Blues' song, doesn't it?)

The difference between what actually is and what you perceive or believe differs only in your interpretation of what, how or by whom it was presented. Your interpretation, in turn, is guided, influenced or determined by your pre-existing beliefs. These pre-existing beliefs can make you vulnerable to scams that prey on those same beliefs.

Why do people fall for scams? Most scams are based on what we want to hear, on what we want to see or on what we want to believe. And deep down inside we all really do want to believe. Even the hardened skeptics have an Achilles' heel somewhere. I'm sure you've heard stories like this before. An author of a book that warns of financial scams and explains ways to prevent them actually becomes a victim of an elaborate financial scam, or a cyber security expert gets hacked. Crumbling credibility aside, the author and the cyber security expert wholeheartedly believed that their advice would successfully safeguard against these scams, and, if their pitch was good, we believed right along with him.

We love to believe. We live to believe. So, whenever the opportunity to fall for some deceptive scheme comes our way we gladly go out of our way to take advantage of some enticing illusion. And afterwards, in the majority of cases, we rationalize to ourselves it wasn't really our fault or, in a very few extreme cases, we convince ourselves it never really even happened. It's kind of a buyer's remorse thing. This mental susceptibility is the basis of the old, "if it sounds too good to be true, it probably is" adage. So it's not too remarkable that people are still so perpetually optimistic they truly believe they can get something for nothing. This is the magician's tent form of convoluted self-pitching.

The Negative Sales Pitch

In the *"Pied Piper's Sonic Flute Sales Pitch Indoctrination and Training Manual,"* you'll find there are a few distinctive types of negative sales pitches. The first and most obvious type deals with the belittlement of a competitor or their products or services. You may know it as the "build yourself up by tearing others down" sales pitch.

Effectively discrediting the competition or planting seeds of doubt can grease the wheels of even a weak sales pitch. This is usually pretty transparent and generally a fairly ineffective approach, except, of course, in politics. People are typically turned off by negativity, even when it's directed at the competition, once again, except in politics.

Another type of negative sales pitch engages a more subtle and effective manipulation technique. It's also known as a negative reverse sales pitch. We all know it's very difficult to convince people they want or need something they're not already searching for. When we attempt to directly impose a sales pitch, all we do is evoke defensive reactions. People react negatively, sometimes unconsciously, by either supporting whatever it is they already own or use or they simply turn off and rebuff everything.

They become predisposed to reject new propositions, proposals or options. With an effective negative reverse sales pitch, people can be "lead to discover for themselves" that a new direction can be beneficial. When people are "lead to discover" a better way, it engages the subject's own "I-came-up-with-it" form of self-pitching.

This turns out to be far more effective than the all too common application of a sales pitch pressure method. People love to buy, but dislike being sold. By redirecting or mimicking a subject's comments, actions, objections or concerns back to them as questions, the subject is left to produce his or her own answers. This allows them to overcome their own reservations or objections. In essence, they answer themselves out of objections and into buying.

There's one other type of "negative sales pitch." In salesmanship, one of the procedural steps is to "qualify" the customer. If the customer isn't qualified financially or is otherwise determined to be unable to fulfill the obligations required of a buyer then the need to proceed is eliminated. This kind of negative sales pitch is more of a disqualifier than a qualifier.

Some folks mentally rebel when they're told they aren't ready for or aren't qualified for a product or service. The subtlety that's inherent in this negative sales pitch is this lack of qualification. This creates a defensive attitude and piques their desire. "What do you mean, I can't have it?" or "What do you mean I'm not good enough?"

Negative selling only works when you develop an even stronger desire because it's something you are unqualified for or simply can't have. Wow, now you're susceptible to that inevitable "bait and switch" price hike. This type negative selling plays on people's insecurities combined with their insatiable desire to fulfill their wants, even if it's something they don't really want.

Selling the Seller

Most people don't realize as much money is made during the buying process as during the selling. Back in my home-building days, just as much of my time was spent negotiating with suppliers and contractors than was spent in construction. If I had bought into the prices they were trying to sell me on, I would have never made a dime. From excavating to installing cabinets, from concrete to lumber and shingles, from gas and electric to plumbing and heating, every minute of labor and every square inch of materials had to be negotiated. The selling that was involved was to counter the sales pitches the suppliers were pushing. Remember, almost everything is negotiable.

I taught my kids early on that the only way you will ever get a deal is to ask for one. If you buy something for a price that anyone else can buy it for, it's not a deal. A seller must be sales-pitched into selling something for less. Remember, they're trying to buy your money with what you want. Your money is valuable because it can be used to buy anything. Their product or service can only be used to buy money.

The Phantom Sales Pitch

Leading people to buy into a sales pitch when they don't even know they're being pitched is a pretty nifty trick. The best example of a phantom sales pitch is brought to you by the entertainment industry. They are masters of leading us to where they want us to go.

The use of applause signs and canned laughter to elicit a response is a fairly common application of this type of ploy. It's utilized to elicit responses from both live and taped television audiences all the time. When a laugh track is used, is it because a gag is truly funny or is it because the producers know when we hear laughter we're unconsciously cajoled into either laughing along with it or accepting the humor as valid? Obviously, the show's creators are telling us it's funny, whether we think it is or not. Remove the laugh track and you quickly realize the validity of the humor is often radically altered. It ties in with the herd mentality of a previous chapter.

Laugh tracks are synthetic reactions that emanate from an artificial herd that we instinctively want to be part of. It's comfortable, it's non-threatening and it leads us in a direction we're expecting and already have a preexisting desire to go.

We are impulsively stimulated to become part of this manufactured herd and laugh right along with them. If we laugh along with the laugh track at something that wasn't really funny have we been deceived? Were we simply gullible when tricked into momentarily believing it was funny just because a prompter said so? "Wait a minute, that wasn't funny. They lied to us." To agree with a nonexistent herd and actually participate in a contrived reaction of fabricated laughter is truly a sales pitch born in the "magician's tent." And besides, our humor-laugh response impulse just wouldn't be the same without a good laugh track.

Things Change

Slight fluctuations in life, nuances in family dynamics, and refinements in relationships are some of the almost unnoticeable influences that lead us onto paths we seldom even notice we're meandering down. Like living with someone closely enough not to notice the changes that ageing hangs on us.

This obviously isn't purposeful deception, or even deception born of intent. But it sure is more comfortable than hacking at the brush to create a singular path to avoid the possibility of deception. All of us are susceptible to deception. When deception is presented in an atmosphere of overwhelming credibility it's nearly impossible not to equate it as truth. When told often enough or when everyone else believes it, sometimes, even a lie becomes truth.

Following Up

The subtle follow-up sales pitch often comes out as one of the most effective sales pitches. Sometimes the follow-up is based in fear: "If you don't take our generous offer, your cousin may have a terrible accident" or the even more effective follow-up where your prized thoroughbred's head ends up in your bed.

My brother lived in a new twin high-rise dorm during his first year of college. The massive amount of trash produced by the dorm residence required daily, or should I say, nightly trash pickups. The containers were huge and the trucks that mechanically lifted them high enough to dump into their waste haulers were huge as well, and really noisy. They were so noisy that many students complained to the university and the trash hauling company. The problem was that they scheduled the pickups at 3:00 a.m. The ongoing complaints were simple attempts to sales pitch them into a daytime pickup. Neither the university nor the trash hauling company bought into these pitches.

Someone, I'm sure I don't remember exactly who, utilizing a subtle follow-up sales pitch, connected a hose to an exterior water valve and dropped the other end into the huge trash bin. The water ran all that afternoon, throughout the evening and through the night, right up until the truck attempted to lift the bin.

I say attempted because about three seconds after the front tires of the truck came off the ground attempting to lift the tons of water, several loud grinding bangs were heard. The front end of the truck smashed back to the ground and loud cursing could be heard. I guess you could say there was a great deal of weight behind this trash-talking follow-up sales pitch. The results were some obvious and obligatory threats to the unknown perpetrators of this dastardly deed followed by a conciliatory buy-in to the not-so-subtle phantom pitch. Daytime trash pickups continue to this very day.

Threats of violence and destruction are acts of intimidation whose sales pitch effectiveness is not lost on the powers that be. From street gangs to major world powers there are sales pitches that promise ramifications if not bought into. Sometimes, negotiations, which are sales pitches with counter pitches, can reconcile threatening or aggressive posturing. Other times, more aggressive, power-based direct action may serve as a more effective counter sales pitch. When major forces attempt to move contradictory major forces the sales pitches can take hostile or violent forms.

Blue Sky, Smilin at Me, Nothing but Blue Sky Do I See
Getting top dollar for hope and possibilities

Ever been sold on something that's based on its potential, probable or possible benefit? That, my friend, is "blue sky." This "blue sky" is generally presented with a proposition very similar to "all you gotta do is." The completion of this "all you gotta do" is really what produces the value. When "all you gotta do" hasn't been completed, you're really paying someone else for your own future efforts that may or may not turn blue sky into reality.

Way back in high school I was told by a guidance counselor that there is no more demanding burden than the obligations imposed by a great potential. "It can only be fulfilled by you and the diligent application of effort."

Talk about "blue sky". Potential what? I knew I was being told or sold something profound. To me, unfortunately, it was blue sky packaged in an even more nebulous blue sky. It was okay though. I merely nodded my head to convey the illusion that I had bought into the warm and loving grand philosophical intent behind whatever it was she was babbling. Its fairly easy to pitch "blue sky" when the subject is completely in the dark.

The best example of a "blue sky" pitch is in buying a business opportunity when the price of the business is based on its possible or potential success. The value of the business is in the effort required to make sure it's successful.

You will seldom find that the price and the value are anywhere close to each other. The difference between the two is that, with "blue sky," you'd actually be paying the seller for the effort you would need to exert in order for the business to be as successful as advertised. Good luck with that.

Brain Trix

The deceptive sales pitch bag of tricks contains these and many more fallacies, misleading tactics and logic flaws that are designed to not only influence perspective subjects and overcome objections in sales pitches but to also gain advantage in negotiations and arguments. You've probably noticed a few of them in presidential debates. Recognizing these when you hear them is a powerful defense against con artists, unscrupulous sales people and your kids when they really want something. You'll also find that social ideologies and dogmas tend to contain a good deal of fallacies and flawed logic, i.e., The Status Quo Sales Pitch of *"I love you just the way you are."*

Why has the US never switched over to the metric system? Why do American men wear suits? Why does landing a menial job require a college education? Why does one spouse continually tolerate the other's incomprehensible behavior? Why do we pay politicians to be in positions of power? Just kidding about the last one. The rest of them are because the sales pitch to keep things as they are is more compelling than the effort implied in a sales pitch to change things. Even when it comes to a point where most people believe things need to change, it's difficult to implement that change.

Expectations

Sales pitches driven by expectation generate promissory buy-ins. While some of this is self-pitching, a great deal goes back to the fear factor. A human's competitive nature is based on positive self-expectation. Those who acquiesce to defeat aren't only drained of competitive nature but of positive self-expectation.

External expectation can motivate through diametrically opposed forces. On the one hand, most people have, at least to some degree, a desire to please others. Whether it's a uplifting boss, an inspirational coach, an encouraging teacher or even the really cute one, the desire to meet or exceed expectations can be an extremely pleasurable motivator. On the other hand, the fear generated by not meeting expectations can be incredibly uncomfortable. Expectation is an implied sale pitch that provides its own motivation. I mean really, what else would you expect from an expectation?

As you can see, many abstract, creative, artful and deceptive forms of sales pitches reside in the magician's tent. The deception exemplified by the Trojan horse sales' pitch worked because it relied on the exploitation of hopeful trust by others in the face of deceptive means driven by malicious intentions. The presentation of the pitch wouldn't have worked without the hopeful trust. Sales pitches based in expectations work because of people's inherent desire to participate. When subtle expectations and directions present conditions of comfort or enjoyment, there's little incentive to restrict one's own participation.

And yes, fun-house mirrors, Sleight of hand and photoshopped images represent but a few of the misleading, brain deceiving, sales pitches that reside in the magician's tent.

Chapter Thirteen
– Using Your Brain Without Losing Your Mind –
We are what we think.
Or do we just think we are?

Think About It

As stated in previous chapters, thinking is a complex manipulation of memories and past perceptions based on immeasurable amounts of constant sensory input. This thinking is then utilized in a vast assortment of mental analysis, interpretation and scrutiny. The eventual result is nothing more than a perpetual continuation of additional perception-based opinions or judgments. This is only one of the reasons any of your opinions that differ from my opinions are obviously wrong. And visa-versa, I'm sure.

Let Your Brain Make the Decisions?

Just as "thinking" is the manipulation, engagement and application of memories, "decision making" is the manipulation, engagement and application of opinions, judgments and beliefs to problems, situations, opportunities and possibilities. From your morning breakfast to your chosen career, from choosing a first friend to choosing a wedding ring, your decisions move you through life's little sales pitch jungle.

Based on everything you've bought into before, it's your decision to either believe or not believe anything, everything or nothing—or any combination thereof. How you choose to utilize and apply your opinions and judgments is the essence of decision making.

The thought process of rejecting a thought process, and how we prevail over the siren temptation of sales pitches, resides in our decision-making capabilities. Only you can choose to accept or reject a sales pitch or its premise. The decisions you make can, and do, determine the direction of your entire system of beliefs. What you do and what you believe are a direct result of the decisions you make. The decisions you make also pretty much determine who you are and what level of comfort or discomfort you are willing to tolerate.

"My God, is that what this book is all about, decision making? Talk about a manipulation and exploitation sales pitch."

Contrary to a lot of wacky old academic scholars, having your brain crammed with a bunch of facts does not, in itself, make you smart; it makes you knowledgeable. Additionally, whenever too much idealism or too many solidified beliefs are mixed in with your bundle of facts, your smart factor diminishes exponentially.

Remember that reality, fact and truth are all antonyms of belief, while knowledge is nothing more than the massive cluster of accumulated memories rattling around in your brain. Thinking, on the other hand, is your brain masterfully manipulating this incalculable mass of memories. Your interpretation and mental manipulation of all these memories, i.e., "thinking," is what shapes and defines your unique and personal perception of reality.

The greater your mastery of memory manipulation, the more in line with reality your beliefs can be, not to mention, how intelligent others will perceive you to be. However, your intelligence and its complement, "your perceived intelligence," differ only on how effectively you are able to pitch or show off your knowledge to others. Your ability to express the results of your brainy exercises to others is the true measure of your perceived intelligence.

Mentally constructing sophisticated and effective solutions to the world's problems without expressing them effectively will only make you smart to you. You can't change the world or reveal your smarts unless you effectively communicate these solutions. In other words, it's not simply what's in your brain that's relevant, it's the skills necessary to successfully articulate and expose that content to the judgment of others.

Successful communication will always be a determining factor in the assessment of your intellectual prowess, scholastic capability, social acceptance and, of course, your ability to convince the really cute one. In other words, if your brain fell in the forest and there was no one there to decipher it, would the thoughts it contains be relevant or meaningful?

People think, believe and conclude in ways they hope will comfort, embellish and enrich their existence. People sales pitch themselves into patterns. These patterns only change when they are in conflict with the judgments of what are believed to be more credible outside sources. The result of the self-pitch vs. the "other's" pitch will always be based on a judgment of the "other's" credibility. And that judgment will most certainly be based on an expected level of comfort. When others judge you, their judgment will be generally based more on your ability to express your thoughts than for the thoughts themselves. Smart is good, but your level of success in life is determined far more by your "sales pitch" ability.

In order to get what you want, get rid of what you don't want, direct and manipulate others or achieve your desired purpose, you must successfully employ "sales pitches." Effectively directed communication = persuasion/manipulation = successful sales pitch.

Is There Really Freedom of Choice, or Just the Belief That There Is?

Free to choose? Do you seriously believe you have a totally objective, unencumbered freedom of choice? What makes you think so? Did someone tell you this? Did they convince you of this? Or do the choices you make come from some deep logical, intuitive or rational thought processes? If it is the latter, has any person, place or thing influenced or prejudiced these thought processes in any way? Of course your answer is: *"No, of course not. I'm certain my choices are completely independent of the beliefs, prejudices and bias that I have built up over a lifetime."* Yea, right.

Your choices are a result of what you've been conditioned to buy into. The only free will you have may very well be to choose which sales pitch you will buy into. Even that choice is based on all of the other sales pitches you have bought into. And what kind of a choice is that?

When exercising freedom of choice, are you merely embracing a sales pitch, employing analytical reasoning or blindly adhering to your beliefs? Are you applying a rational thought process or mimicking dogma-based philosophies? Is a free will really free, or is there a price? Or has your free will been internally obviated by the accumulated beliefs that direct or dictate your choices? People's decision-making capabilities are often hindered because they rarely apply rational thought, logic and reasoning to beliefs, bias and prejudice-based sales pitches. And seldom do they make rational and coherent decisions with intellect rather than opinions and beliefs.

Now factor into this the reality that no human being has ever been able to come up with anything that's universally right or universally wrong. Why? Right and wrong aren't indisputable facts; they are value judgments. It is your own cluttered brain's interpretation of circumstances that inhibits you from being truly free to choose which is which. So, any actual freedom of choice is proportional to the capacity and desires to apply rational thought to all options, without the encumbrances of imposed obligations, threats, coercions or other internal or external persuasively influential forces.

The reality is, we all are simply the innocent captives of an illusion of both a freedom and a free will that have been sales-pitched to us. We are all somewhat predisposed to buy into the thoughts or opinions of others whenever they potentially provide the possibility of personal comfort. Skepticism usually fades rather quickly if we can't shoot holes in the logic or are just too mentally lazy to scrutinize other views.

People believe their perceptions are more acute or that their mind operates on a higher level. Yet, willfully, they still accept interpretations or explanations of truth or facts from questionable sources they themselves deem credible or trustworthy (or ones they're sympathetic to). Most folks not only welcome the thoughts and opinions from these sources, they willingly allow them to weave themselves into the fabric of their already biased mind. This process serves as a comfortable reinforcement of already predisposed beliefs, opinions or prejudices. What we have here are beliefs that lack scrutiny or skepticism.

When people disbelieve, they do so with total and unequivocal scrutiny and skepticism. Witness the current political polarity. Disbelief of candidates in the opposing parties is palpable. This intensity of doubt is reserved for those whom we vehemently disagree with. Disbelief doesn't make you right simply because you find fault with the logic, reason or the conclusions of others, it only makes you think you're right. Just because you can't shoot holes in someone else's theory doesn't make it a fact or a reality. It just makes it a perception you find difficult to disprove. And, as such, it can potentially become a new-shared belief.

It can then evolve into a new basis for your arguments, thought process or belief system, until, of course, it is altered by, what you believe to be, a better logic pattern born of your own direct sensory input (or another belief-based sales pitch).

Deciding Is Such a Difficult Decision

Do you base your decisions entirely on what you believe? If not, what have you been basing your decisions and value judgments on? What decisions have truly come directly from your mind without going through your BS filter or your preconceptions?

Thought, my friend, is, as stated before, simply a manipulation of your memories. And your memories are nothing more than a product of your cumulative sensory input. How you manipulate these memories initially result in your personal perception of reality, your conclusions and, consequently, your decisions. Your database of info is ever expanding. Unfortunately, the decisions you make are based on your previously entrenched opinions and beliefs along with the gobbledygook you have accumulated in your database. And you now know where your entrenched opinions and beliefs came from—a lifetime of sales pitches. Knowing this frees you to engage and apply your mind in the practice of thinking rationally.

Congratulations, you're thinking now, except maybe for that annoying interference constantly emanating from your opinions. Now, if all you had in your mind were facts, you could form your own sanitized and disinfected opinions. No value judgment, no favorite, no ranking or comparison. You're tempted now to believe you developed them on your own. Wrong again, think-meister. You believed someone who told you how they believe. You found a little comfort in their beliefs, and now, with a little scrutiny, based on other beliefs that you've previously bought into, you justify their belief. Voila, armed with their belief, you are now just a little less smart than you were before.

Think and You Won't Believe It

Question everything, including your own interpretations and conclusions. Only when you understand that everything is a sales pitch will you truly be able to objectively analyze motives or validity, and begin to think objectively. Unfortunately, human beings are endowed with some pretty unique and troubling characteristics: insecurity, uncertainty and self-doubt to name just a few. Most of these physiognomies leave us incredibly susceptible to sales pitches. Short of employing critical defense mechanisms, pitch deflecting training and analytical thinking, there is not much we can do to protect ourselves. We are most vulnerable when we're not, at the very least, just a little skeptical.

Most of us believe without thinking too much about it. We believe so fully in what we gain through each of our five senses that we automatically transfer these beliefs to our interpretation of this input. We then justify those beliefs by making them our opinions. When most of that sensory input is in the form of a sales pitch most of the resulting opinions are the proverbial castles in the sand. Yet we consider these opinions to be truth, fact and, worse yet, reality. Thoughtful analysis can require time and effort, but injudicious beliefs can impair your individuality, negatively influence your behavior and even adversely affect the very nature or direction of your life.

Achieving a pure uncompromised thought process, i.e., true unadulterated "thinking" is the second hardest thing most people ever do. "Doing" comes in third. "Thinking" and "doing" at the same is by far the most difficult. (*There are those who could effectively dispute the correct order of the second and third.*)

Have you ever questioned your own beliefs? I mean have you ever really sat down and asked yourself where your beliefs came from and why you hold them so closely. Everyone is a moral person—within the context of his or her own beliefs. As human beings, we really don't seem to have a problem questioning someone else's beliefs. It's a lot tougher with our own. These are sacred. These are far too dear to question.

After all, don't our beliefs come from our own observations, judgments and conclusions or from the observations of those whom we love or trust? Absolutely not, they come from the accumulation of a lifetime of buying into sales pitches and self-pitches. Remember the "crap" in first chapter? To this point, in all of our lives we've amassed, retained and embraced enough "crap" to completely immobilize our brains.

Why are you so committed to what you believe? Is it because an unquestioned belief is just so convenient or is it because it is too uncomfortable or personally threatening to question the validity of your beliefs.

Okay, okay, I know that subjecting yourself to the agony of confronting the validity of your beliefs could make you just a bit uncomfortable. So, every once in a while, simply apply a bit of your analytical skills instead of just believing.

We are all a product of everything that we have been exposed to. The manipulation of the memories of all that we've been exposed to is the ultimate source of our opinions. It is said that there is nothing new under the sun. There is only an ever-expanding complexity of thought combinations and thus a never-ending source of new sales pitches.

You don't need to be a complete cynic to realize there are very few absolute truths, facts, certainties or realities. Conversely, there is an infinite supply of interpretations, theories, opinions, beliefs, judgments and conclusions. The former are almost void of sales pitches while the latter are the result of, are based on and are almost entirely comprised of sales pitches. So sort it out and think before you buy into what's out there. Believe me when I tell y'all, it really is all just a sales pitch.

Questioning whatever is presented as reality, truth or fact, is a human being's responsibility. Response is root word for both responsible and responsibility, and their all yours.

Ubiquitous Yet Quixotic Advice

Before taking advice, consider the source. Is any of the source's background, intellect or experience credible or even pertinent to your needs? What is the advisor's motive? Is it to warn you, is it to help you in a direction, is it to subliminally threaten you or is it to motivate you? Are the intentions behind the advice kind and generous or is it menacing or intimidating. Remember, advice is just another sales pitch to be bought into. "Let the buyer beware" was ever thus.

One must constantly employ measured scrutiny and acknowledge the possibility of rejecting or revising a thought process in order to prevail over the perpetual temptation of sales pitches. None of us really and truly need to believe, we just believe we do. Don't just believe, question all the answers, be objective and seek out the problems the solutions create. Always be kindhearted and depend more on thinking and doing than on buying into opinions and beliefs.

We humans today are just a little backwards. We tend to define our facts based on our beliefs, which is where the flaws within our opinions resonate. Beliefs and baseless opinions are treacherous, relentless and unyielding slayers of truth, reason, facts and even reality. Because humans employ their abilities to warp and twist facts and reality into biased dogmas and philosophies, the facts and reality are what become distorted.

To a human being, one's own beliefs are self-perceived, then conveyed as truths, facts, and realities—and, unfortunately, they're also incorrectly perceived as correct. Beliefs held too tightly can and often do, warp perceptions of reality. The bottom line is that reality never changes, only our perceptions of it. This is a function of effective sales pitches and our vulnerability to them.

There are four major characteristics that humans have that distinguish us from nearly all other species: A protruding chin, opinions, theories and beliefs. Where do you suppose that leave us on the evolutionary scale when three out of four of these are almost always incorrect? Voltaire summed it up with his observation: "Opinion has caused more trouble on this little earth than plagues or earthquakes."

Don't succumb to the conclusions or arguments of an intelligent person based purely on your perception of their intellectual prowess. The more intelligent the human being is, the better equipped he or she is in proclaiming and defending their belief-based facts. It doesn't make their beliefs any more accurate, just more eloquent. The best decisions are derived from a balance of intellectual and emotional considerations applied with the ridged scrutiny of a kind and well-intentioned mind and heart.

Evolutionary Thinking

Human beings are comfort-seeking creatures. The basic satisfaction of needs is the primary source of comfort: food shelter safety, companionship, sense of belonging or acceptance by others and, of course, security. Satisfying a need or desire for control, self-improvement, amorous or non-procreation sex and self-fulfilling wants can provide a secondary level of comfort. All of these are targets, objectives, sources, foundations, basis as well as the purpose of and the driving force behind sales pitches. While sales pitches can assist us in satisfying our needs, wants, desires and aspirations, they can also convince, cajole, persuade, pressure, coax, entice, induce, seduce and even force, coerce and deceive us. The evolution of the human race began with a process of natural selection based on survival of the fittest and only the strong survive.

Evolution has brought mankind to new paradigm where "survival of the fittest" no longer reflects the manifestation of a human being's physical prowess. Now true strength lies in non-physical power and control. The most evolved members of our species are those who have developed the most effective communication skills along with the sales pitch aptitude and the mental agility required to influence, manipulate and direct the beliefs of others.

A Few Universal Maxims For Human Life On Earth

Whenever someone says: "All you gotta do is ..." know that it's really and truly never all you gotta do.

The cumulative IQ of any decision-making group is inversely proportional to the number of people in that group.

When anyone says: "... to be perfectly honest ..." or "I have to be honest with you," everything they say afterward should be suspect.

When a salesperson offers: "How can I help you today?" It really means, "How can you help me today?"

Every solution creates new problems and every answer creates new questions. There never has, nor will there ever be an end to this self-perpetuating paradigm.

Thinking is a human being's second most challenging and complicated bodily function, and. It is just behind simultaneously thinking and doing.

Chasing your dreams is infinitely more satisfying than actually catching them.

The cruelest suffering a sadist can inflict on a masochist is to deny her the pain she seeks. Saying "no" hurts and satisfies one, the other or both.

The only thing you ever truly own is what you can protect from being taken. This includes your freedom and any semblance of control you may think you have over it.

Giving without sacrifice isn't truly giving. Nor is giving with expectations of returns.

Only a fool plays poker with friends he repeatedly loses to; friends who are bought with money are only loyal to the money.

It's often difficult to put into words the importance of a good vocabulary.

You can't learn to swim without getting wet.
You can't ever come back if you never leave.
You can't succeed if you never try.

The only place that absolutely everyone makes it to is the very end of life.

The only way to never get hurt is to never care.

Sometimes you have to go through a lot of no ones before you find the right someone.

The only way to get where you want to go is in the driver's seat. If you're just a passenger, you're merely getting taken for a ride, and nobody really likes to get taken.

Every journey does not begin with a single step. Most journeys begin with a purpose, a direction or a goal. If you don't know where you want to end up, a first step serves no purpose, so there's no reason to take it.

When you question the answers and acknowledge the problems that solutions create, you will eventually find some degree of truth.

Beyond survival, there's no greater burden than the expectations your boundless potential creates.

Genuine commitment to unconditional love is the complete submission to a lifetime of care and devotion to another.

Personal opinion is something all humans have in common. In spite of our enthusiastic tenacity to maintain the superiority and correctness of our opinions, our opinions are seldom, if ever, either superior or correct.

The biggest occupational hazard is to settle for the wrong occupation.

Most people spend the majority of their time going nowhere in their futile effort to get somewhere.

Everyone is sorry for what they've done after they've been caught.

All people are moral within the narrow context of their own beliefs.

When endeavoring to accomplish such golden things, you'll find the gold hidden in the trying is worth more than any found in the results.

Accepting responsibility for delinquent or careless actions without being subject to consequences or ramifications has little or nothing to do with actually taking responsibility.

The choice of freedom cannot exist without the freedom of choice.

Live your life like you don't need the money.
Speak your heart and mind as if no one is listening.
Give of yourself like you've never been hurt.

Unless your intention is benevolence, don't do unto others that which you'd have others do unto you; their tastes are most likely not the same as yours.

Afterword

Be the puppet master, not the puppet. If you listen carefully to what they're saying, you can tell them what they want to hear and convince them that you're right. This can become the leash that allows you to lead them wherever you want.

When you're being sales-pitched, it's like baby food, and it is always an option to slap your hand into the pitch and splatter it all over their curtains. The word "no" can be more powerful than any sales pitch.

Always allow for a little give and take in your giving and taking. Remember: the beliefs we cling to are nothing more than personally filtered interpretations of illusions that we believe we perceive.

As parsing these words to entwine with thine life doth lie beyond the realm of all skills of which I am imbued, the task I leave for your triumph is indeed as formidable. For this life art one grim and glorious scene you needs must do alone.

Simply Sold
Our Sales Pitched Lives

We are swayed, prompted, enticed and cajoled
Into perceiving and believing all we've been told
We've been lured and coaxed into the fold
Of buying into beliefs that we've been sold
We've been studied, inspected, researched and polled
We've been mentally shoved and shrewdly controlled
We are deceived with promised pots of gold
When ours never comes, we're left in the cold
We attempt to resist by becoming bold
But yield to wanting more than we hold
And covet once more all things we behold
Until buying into pitches finally gets old
Like stale birthday cakes beginning to mold

By David T. Garland III

About the Author

Dave's experience runs the gamut from sales manager of a nationwide shipping and distribution company to owner of a nationally distributed greeting card company. He has also been a very successful custom homebuilder and real estate investor. He currently runs 'Garland Custom Strategies', a consulting company with a client list that ranges from individual business owners to corporations. Dave is also an accomplished sculptor, screenwriter and author.

CPSIA information can be obtained
at www.ICGtesting.com
Printed in the USA
FSOW01n0651010717
35796FS

9 781943 650507